GEEKY LEGO® CRAFTS

Author, Model Maker, and Designer:
David Scarfe

Editor: Lucienne O'Mara
Photographer: Andy Pickford
Cover designer: Ana Bjezancevic

First published in Great Britain in 2015 by LOM ART,
an imprint of Michael O'Mara Books Limited,
9 Lion Yard, Tremadoc Road, London SW4 7NQ
www.mombooks.com

For information on distribution, translation, or bulk sales,
please contact No Starch Press, Inc. directly:
No Starch Press, Inc., 245 8th Street, San Francisco, CA 94103
phone: 415.863.9900; info@nostarch.com; www.nostarch.com

A catalog record of this book is available from the Library of Congress.

ISBN: 978-1-59327-767-3

2 4 6 8 10 9 7 5 3 1

Printed in China

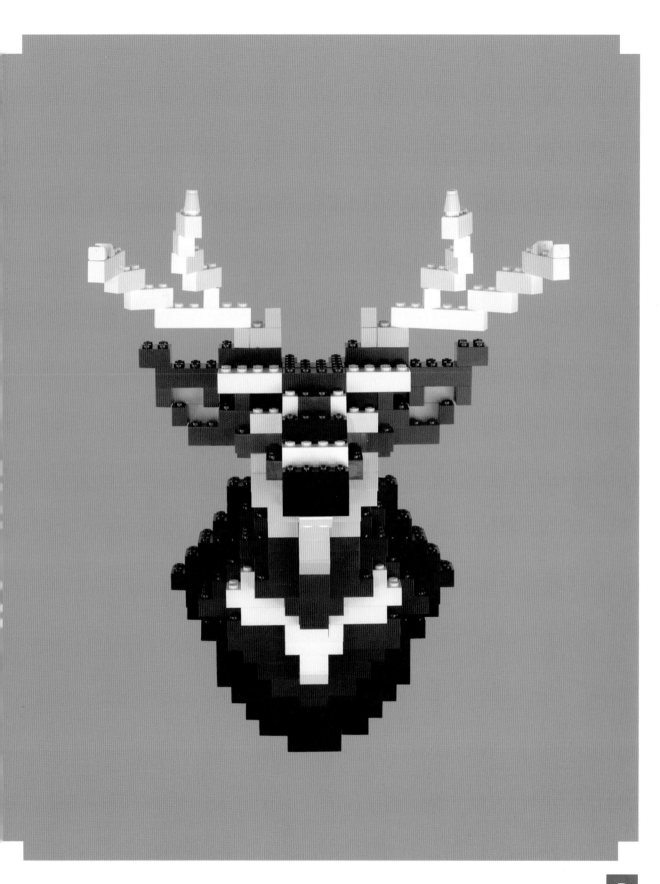

INTRODUCTION

We all loved building with LEGO bricks when we were young, so why stop? This book is for everyone who wants a little inspiration to keep on building!

Whether you want to brighten up someone's car with some "fuzzy" dice or make a set of floppy disk coasters, these projects are fun to build and will bring a little nostalgic cool to your home.

Both practical and retro, these crafts range from quick-and-easy builds to challenging designs that will satisfy even the experienced builder. Between the red-hot flaming toast rack and a wall-mounted deer head, there's plenty to try. Let's brick it!

RATING

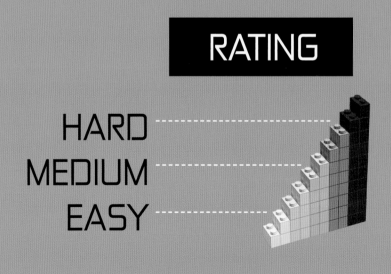

HARD ------------------------

MEDIUM ------------------------

EASY ------------------------

CONTENTS

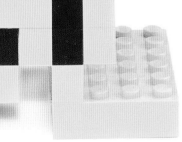

A 1980s arcade classic turned handy stationery holder – what could be better? Save your desk from an invasion of clutter and add a little nostalgia to your working day.

5x
2x
8x
6x
2x
14x
4x
4x
4x
12x
1x
1x

4x
4x
2x
7x
6x
15x
3x
16x
3x
2x

4x
6x
2x
4x
8x
8x
24x
2x
4x
8x

BLUE INVADER

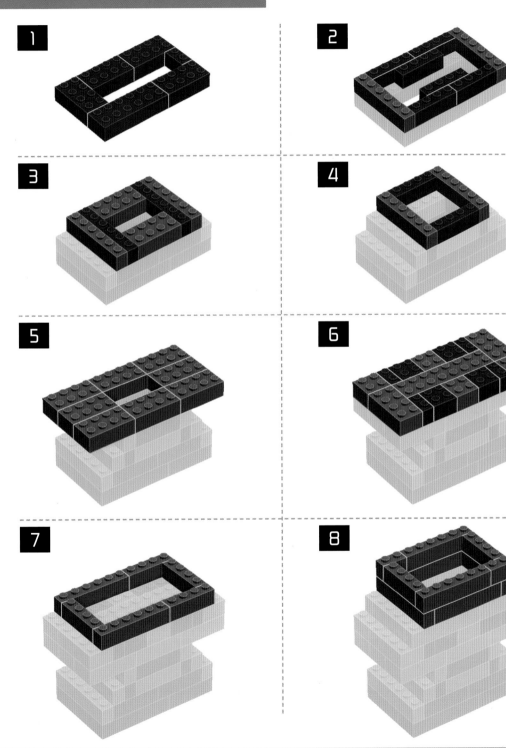

YELLOW INVADER

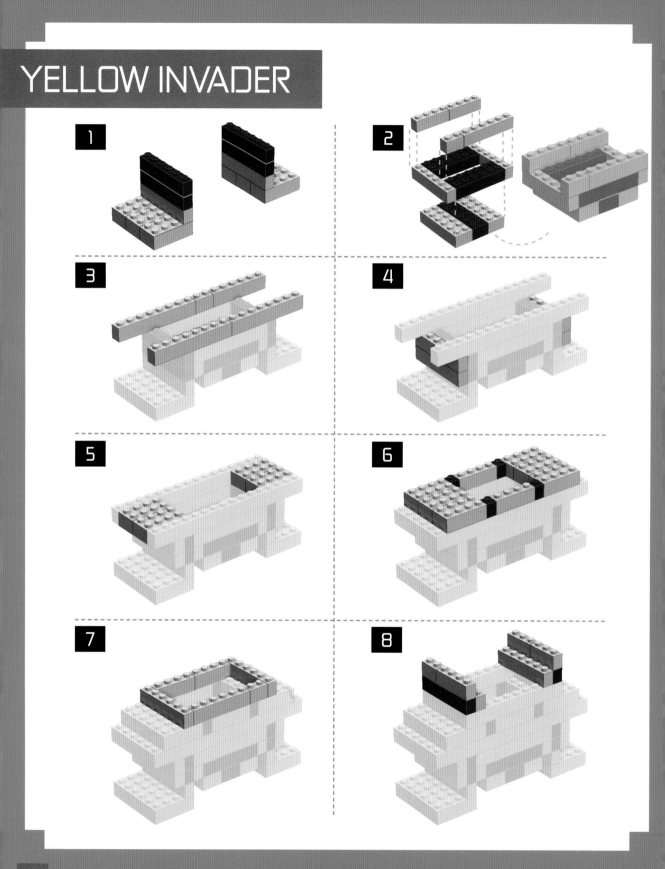

RED INVADER

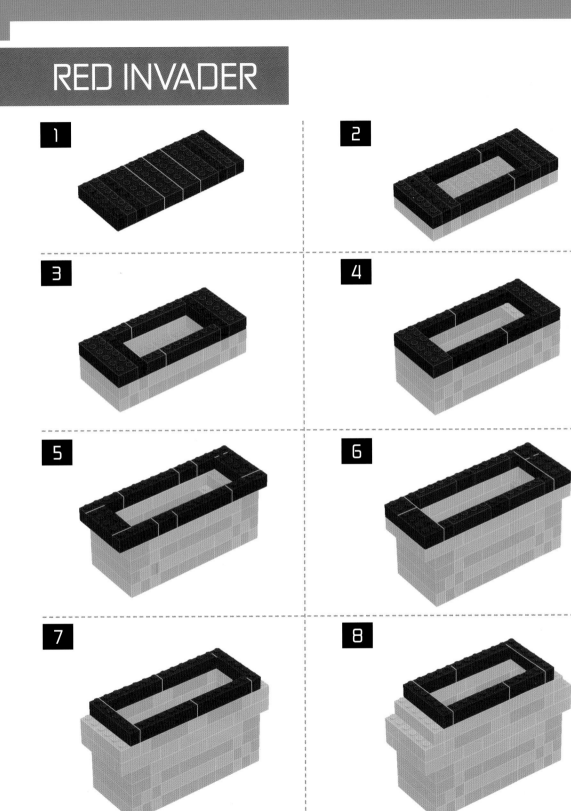

CURSOR BOOKENDS

I THINK, THEREFORE I AM

A CLASSICAL EDUCATION

I WANDERED LONELY AS A CLOUD...

AN APPLE A DAY

I BEFORE E (EXCEPT AFTER C)

I USED TO KNOW THAT

REMEMBER, REMEMBER (THE FIFTH OF NOVEMBER)

SPILLING THE BEANS ON THE CAT'S PYJAMAS

I USED TO KNOW THAT: ENGLISH

I USED TO KNOW THAT: MATHS

Sick of waiting for a web page to load? Tired of pointing and clicking all day? Turn your frustration into a set of bookends that fill your home with a bit of cyber cool.

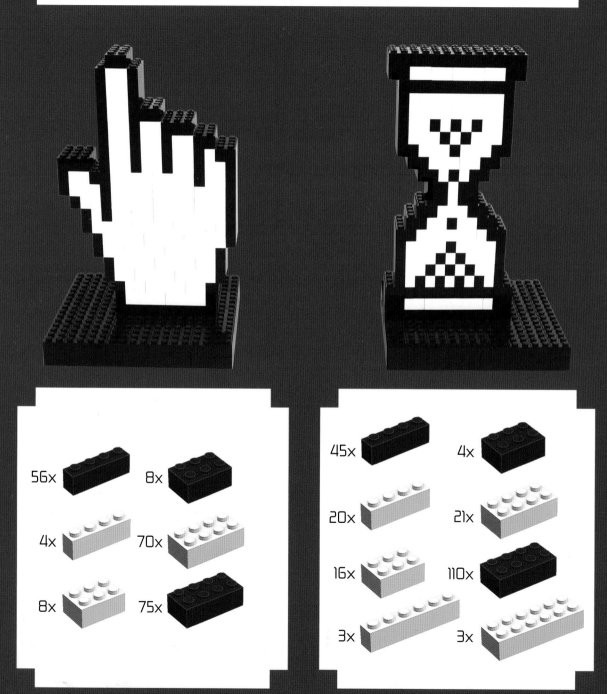

56x

8x

4x

70x

8x

75x

45x

4x

20x

21x

16x

110x

3x

3x

EACH BASE

1

2

x2 of everything

3

4

5

6

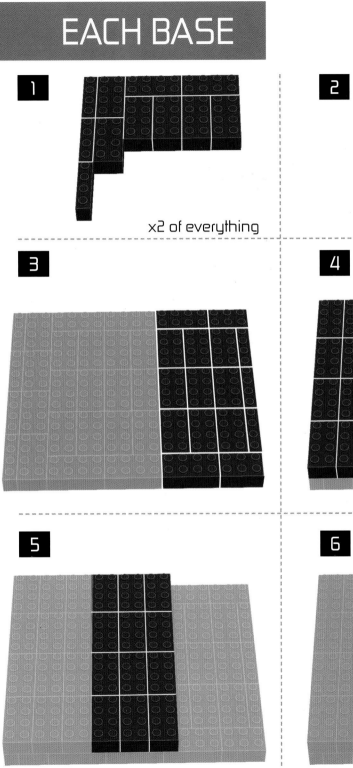
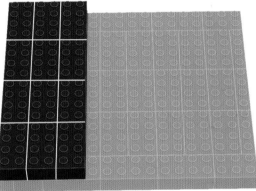
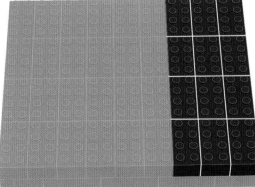

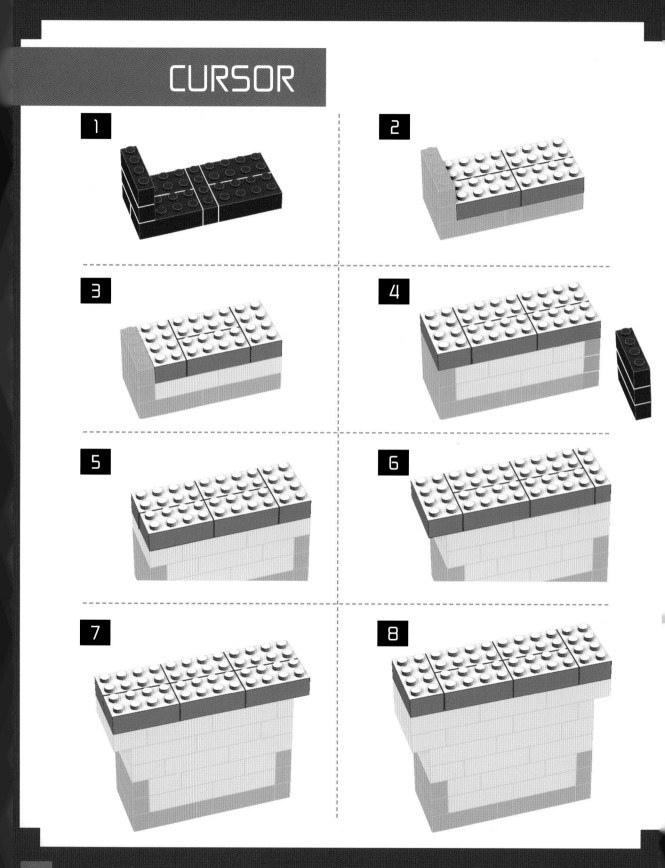

9

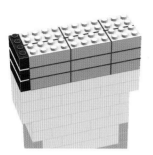

10

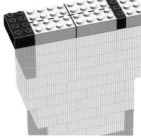

11

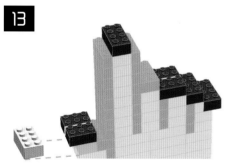

12

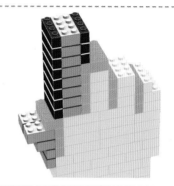

13

15

14

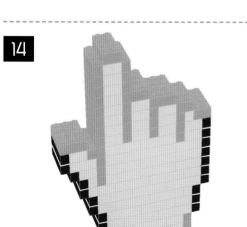

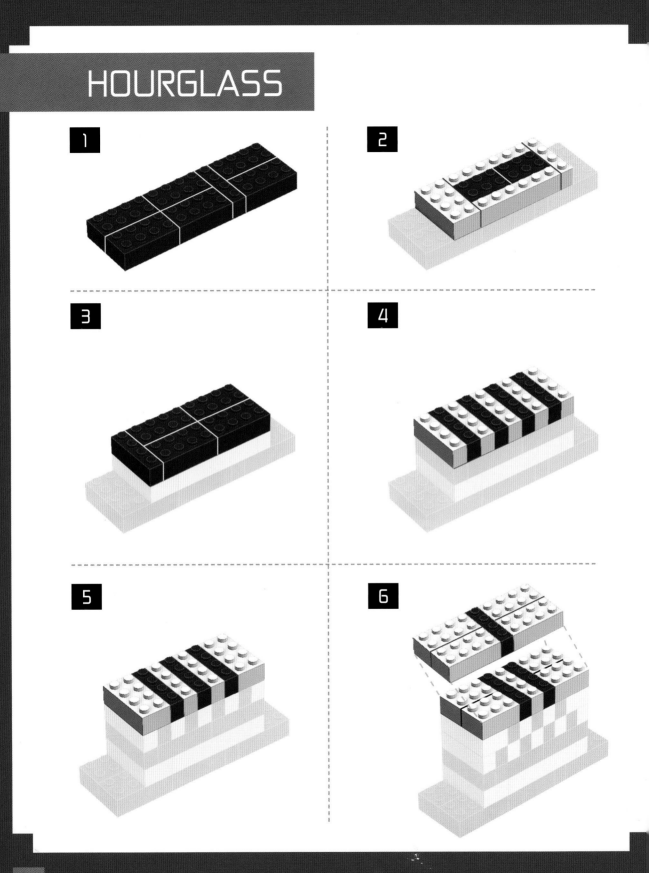

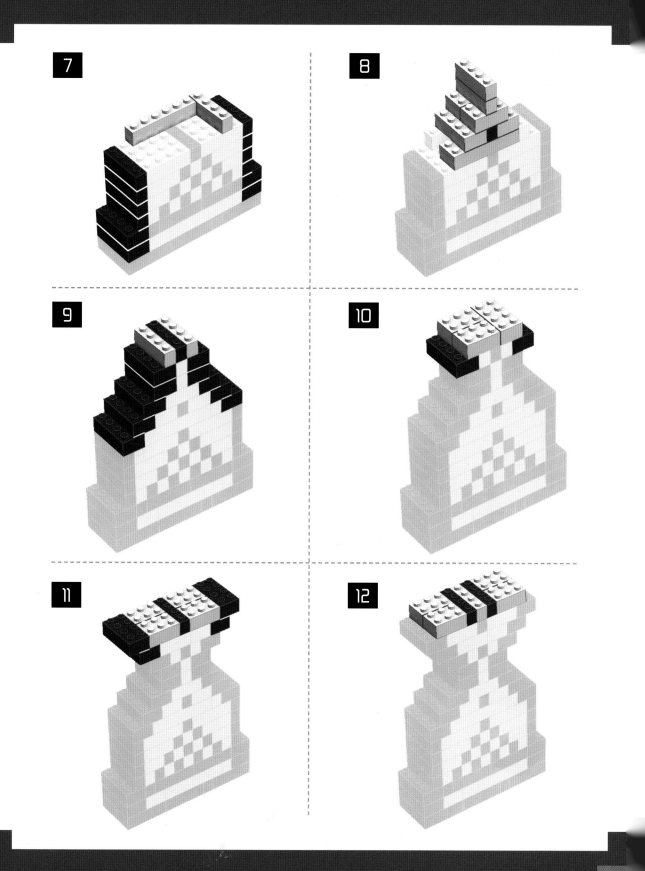

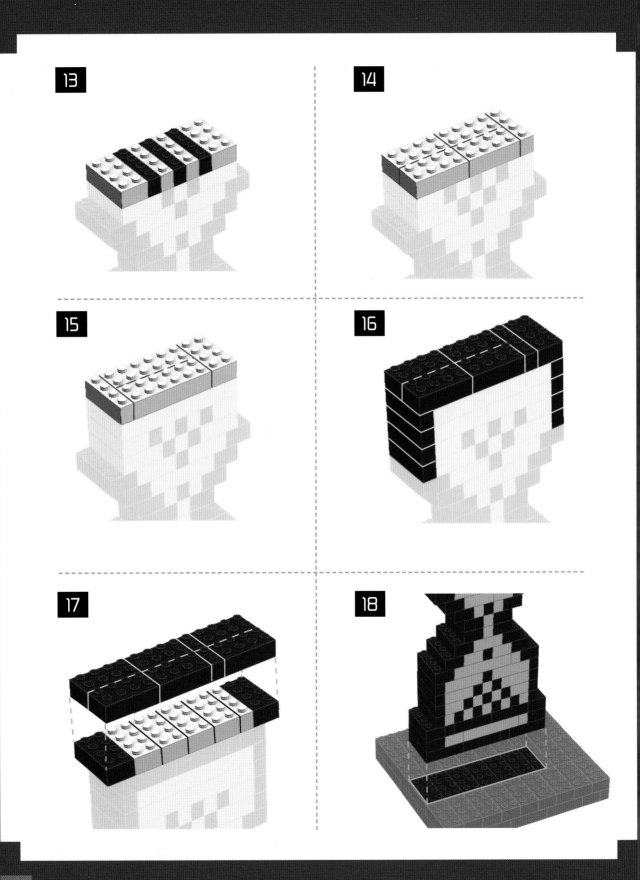

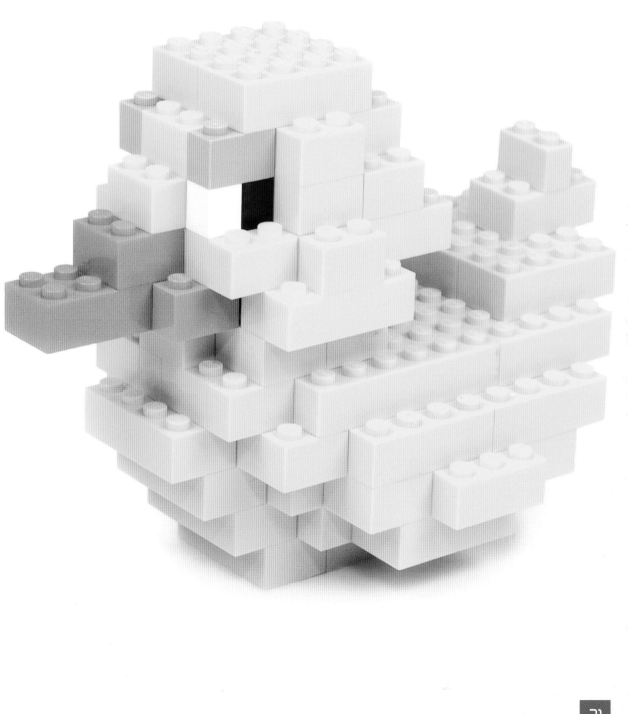

A perfect addition to bath time, this rubber ducky will take you back to those childhood bath times after a long, hard day. Just watch out where he goes—some of those corners are a little sharp. Ouch!

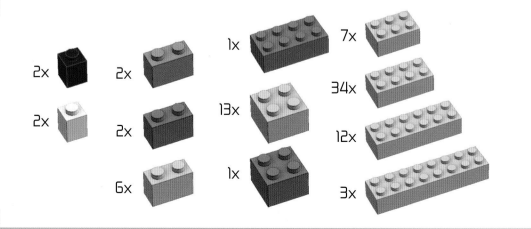

2x

2x

2x

2x

6x

1x

13x

1x

7x

34x

12x

3x

THE HEAD

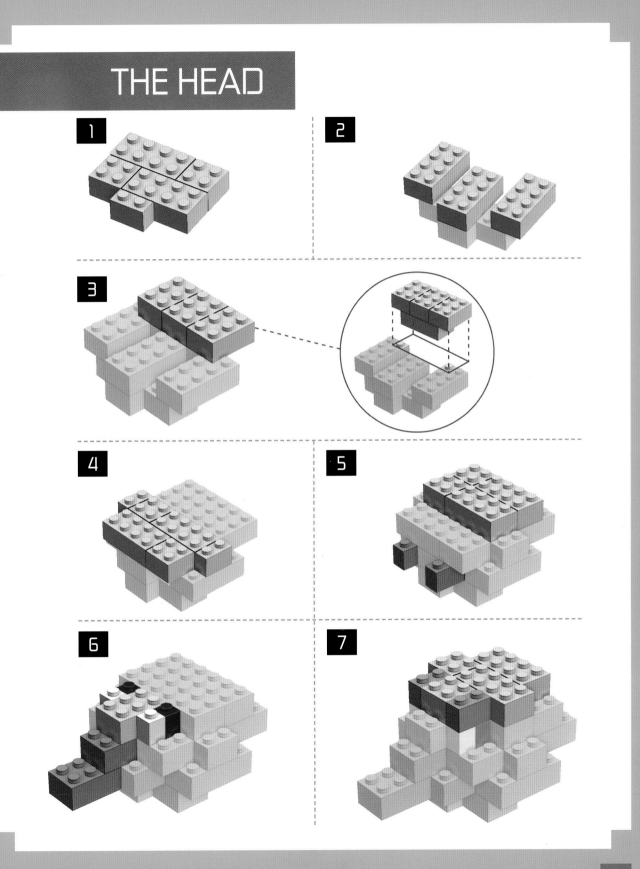

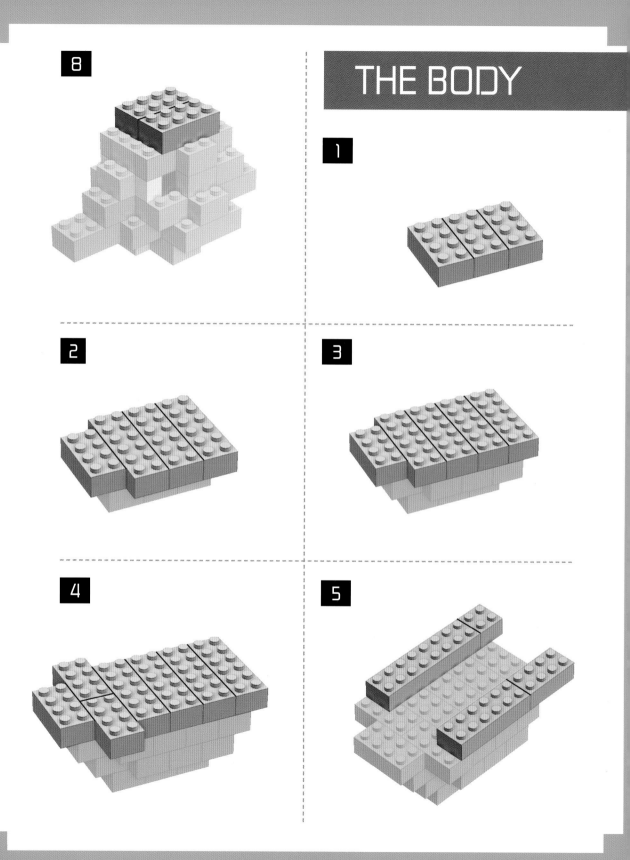

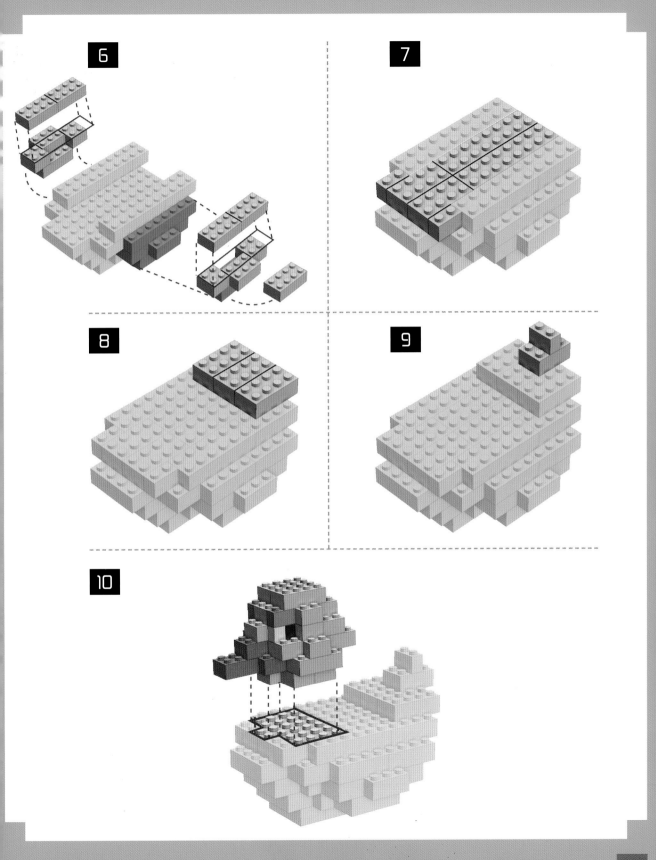

Time to bring these back into fashion. Ideal for any home in need of a little 1960s charm. Don't forget to add a lava lamp and beaded curtain for full effect.

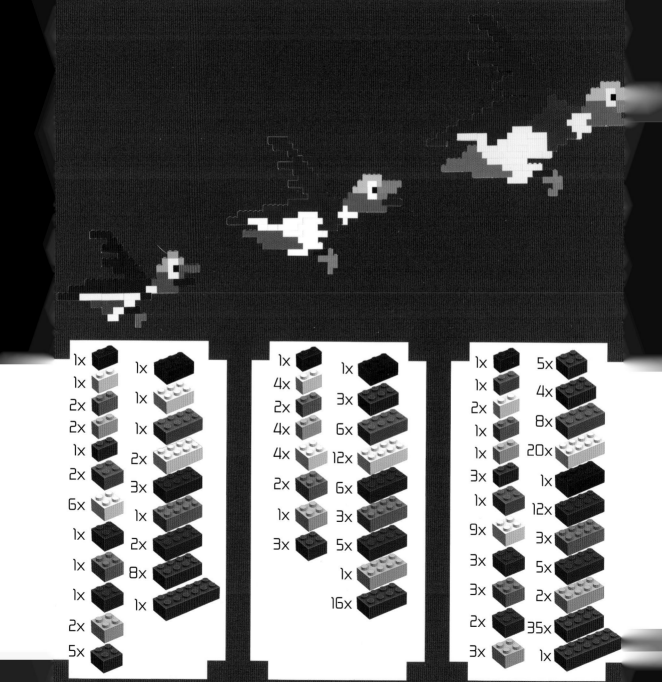

SMALL DUCK

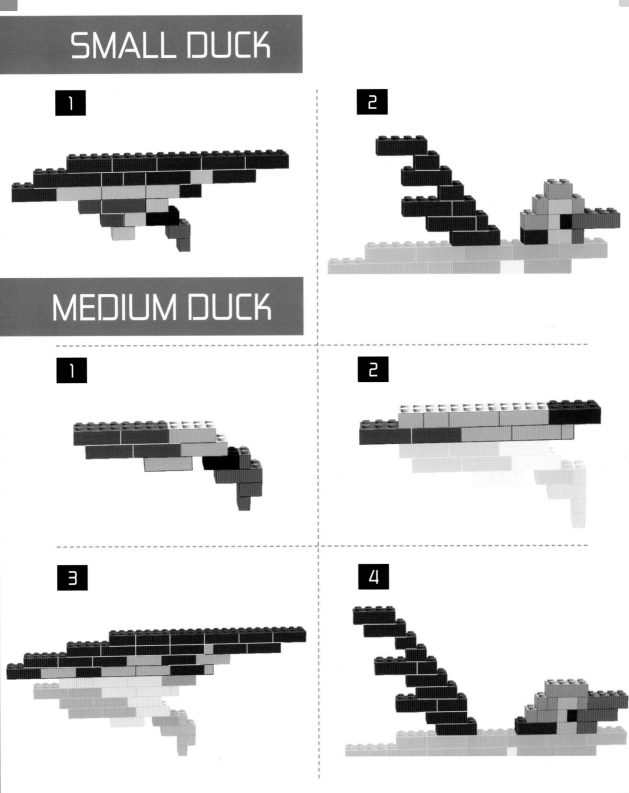

1

2

MEDIUM DUCK

1

2

3

4

LARGE DUCK

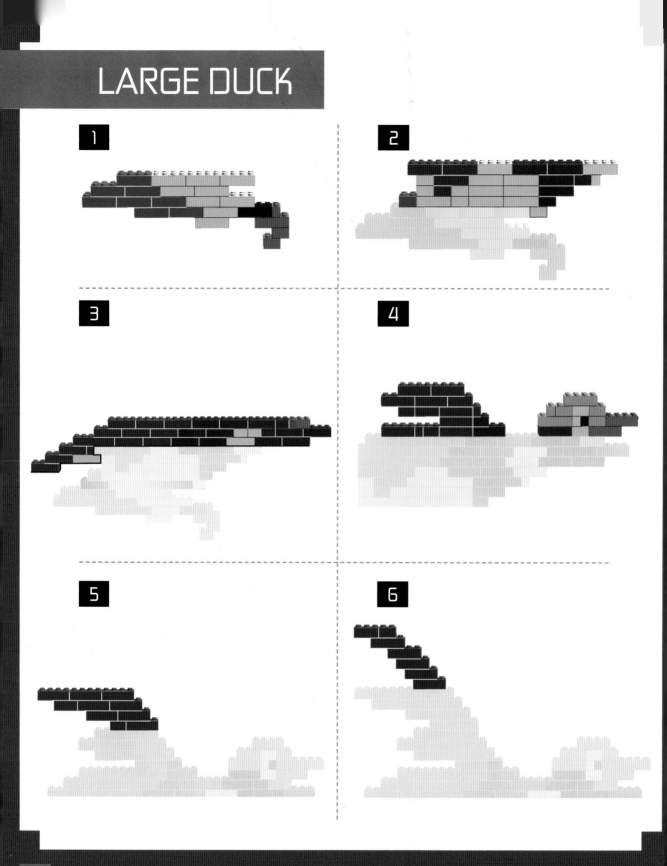

CHRISTMAS DECORATIONS

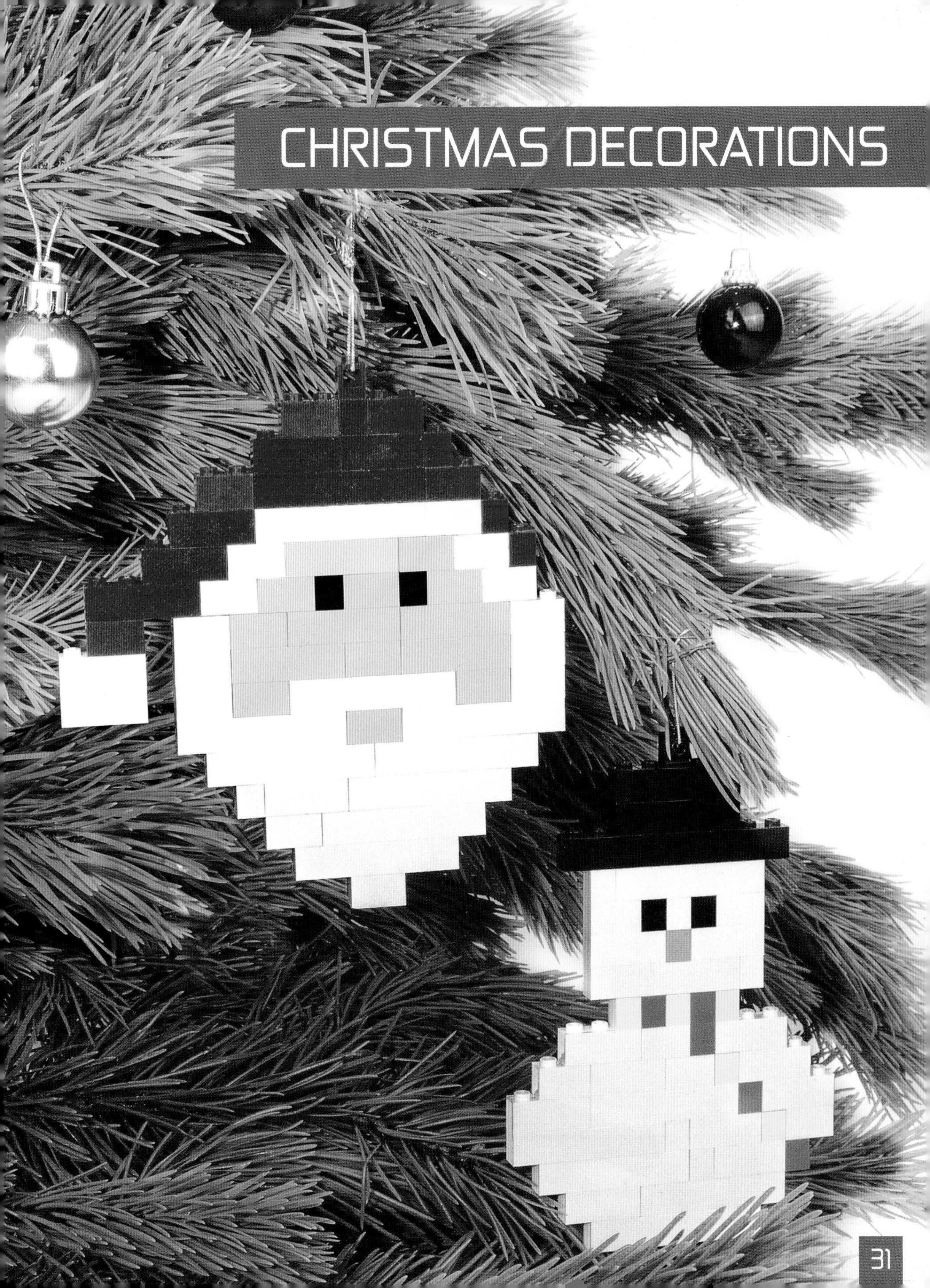

Give your tree a personal touch with these Santa and snowman decorations. Easy to make, they are a perfectly pixelated addition to any Christmas.

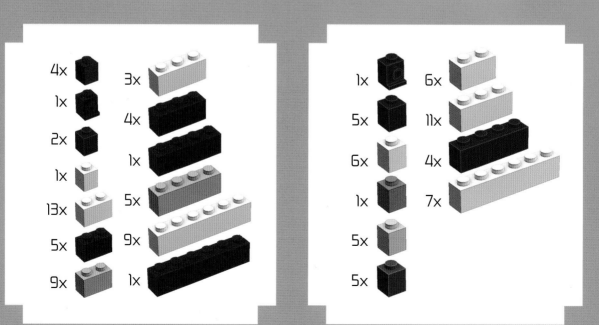

SANTA

1

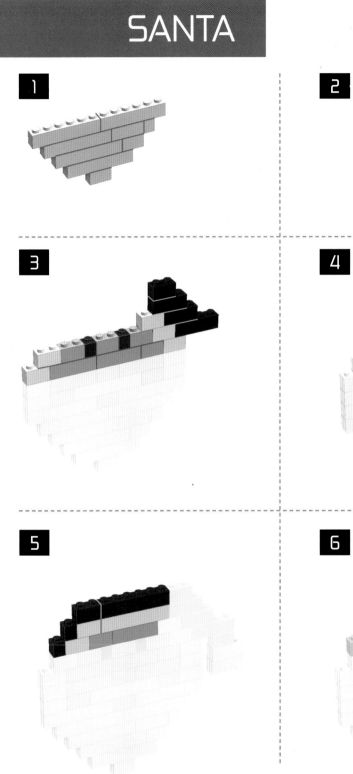

2

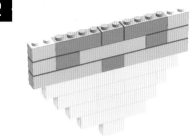

3

4

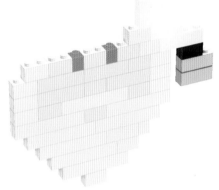

5

6

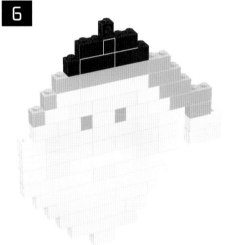

SNOWMAN

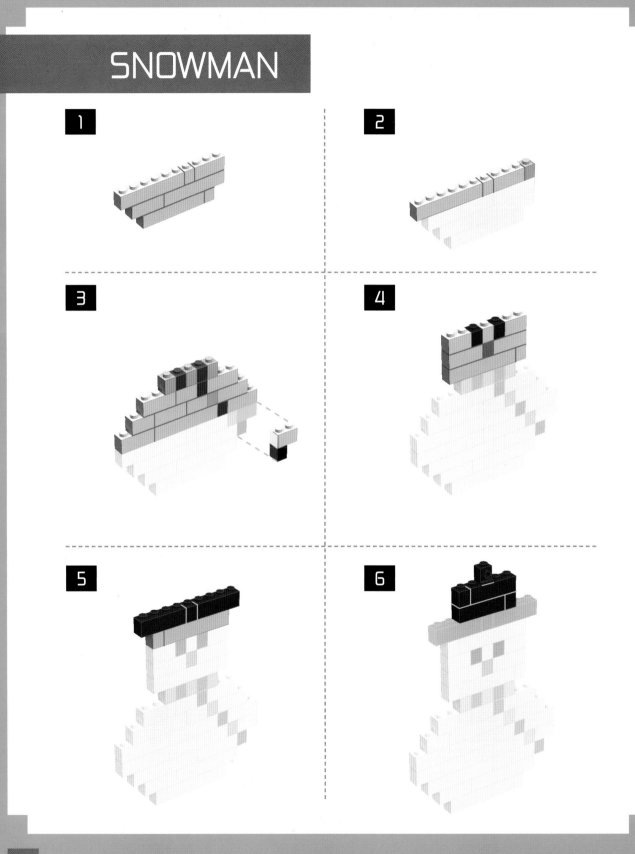

Keep your toast nice and warm with this flaming-hot rack. Just watch your fingers!

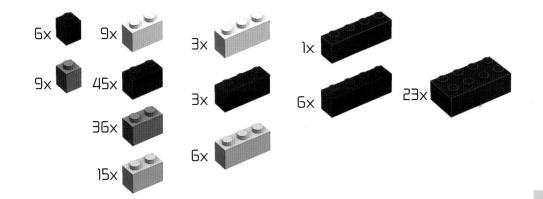

6x   9x   3x   1x

9x   45x   3x   6x   23x

36x   6x

15x

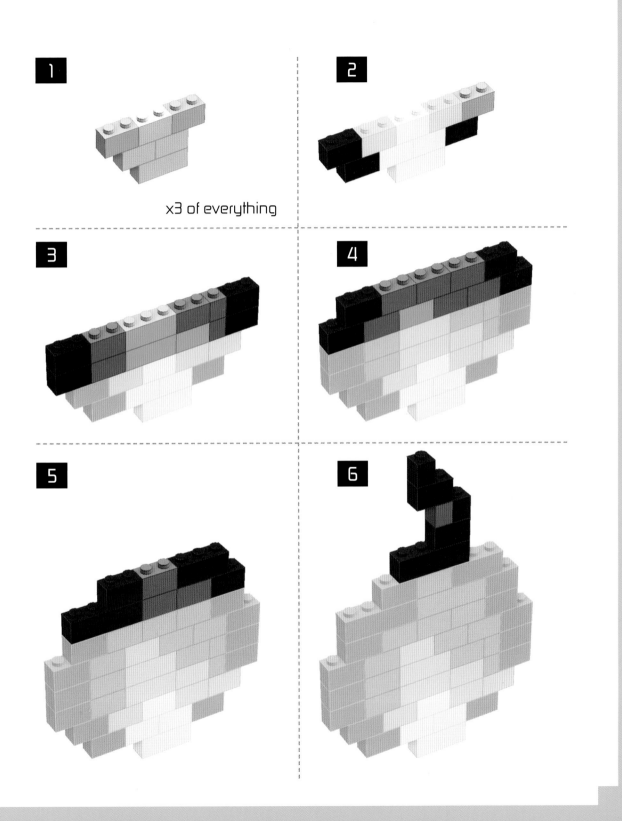

x3 of everything

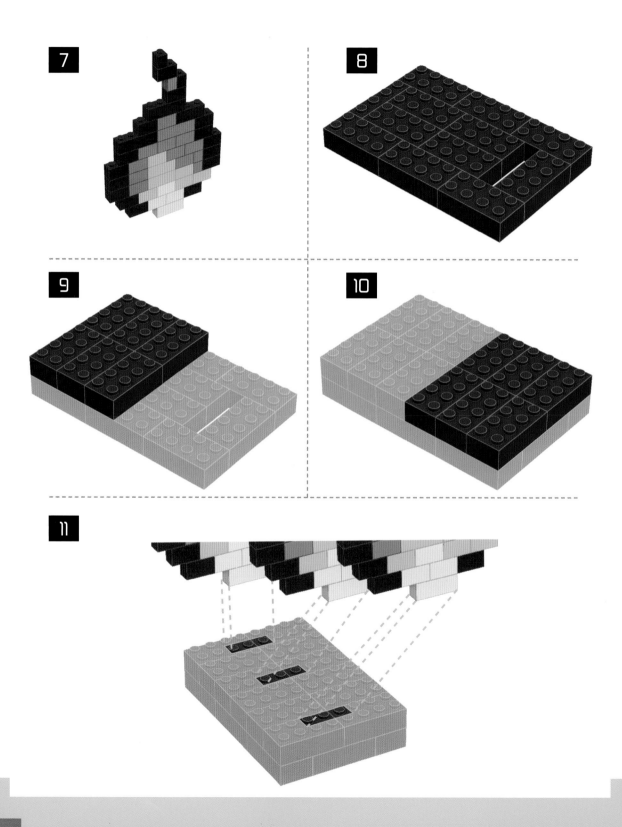

BRAIIIIINNNSSS! Where better to store your pencils than poked into the brain of a reanimated human corpse? Be the envy of your friends with your own Night of the Living Lead.

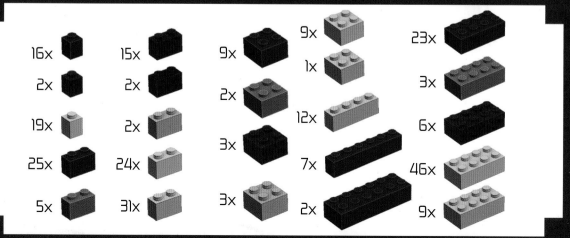

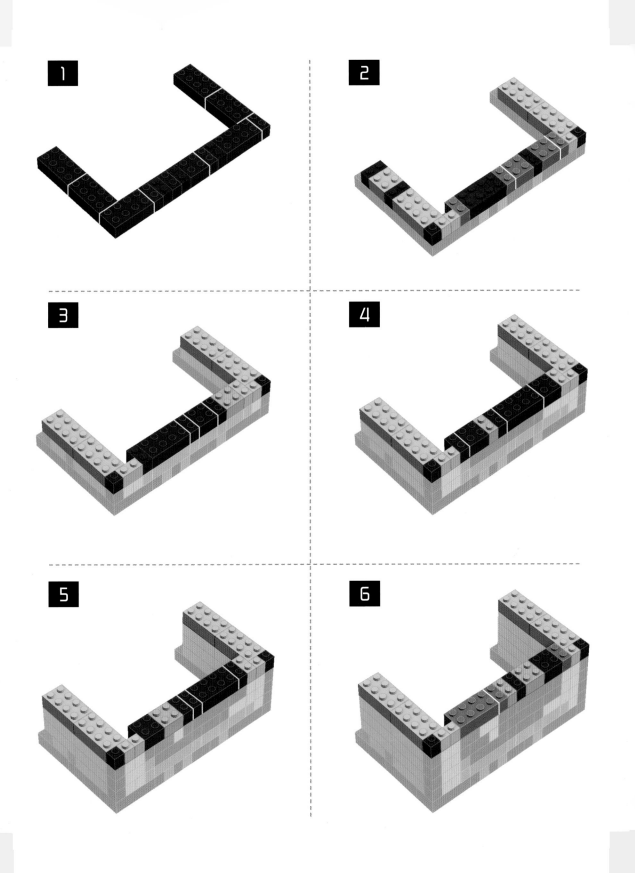

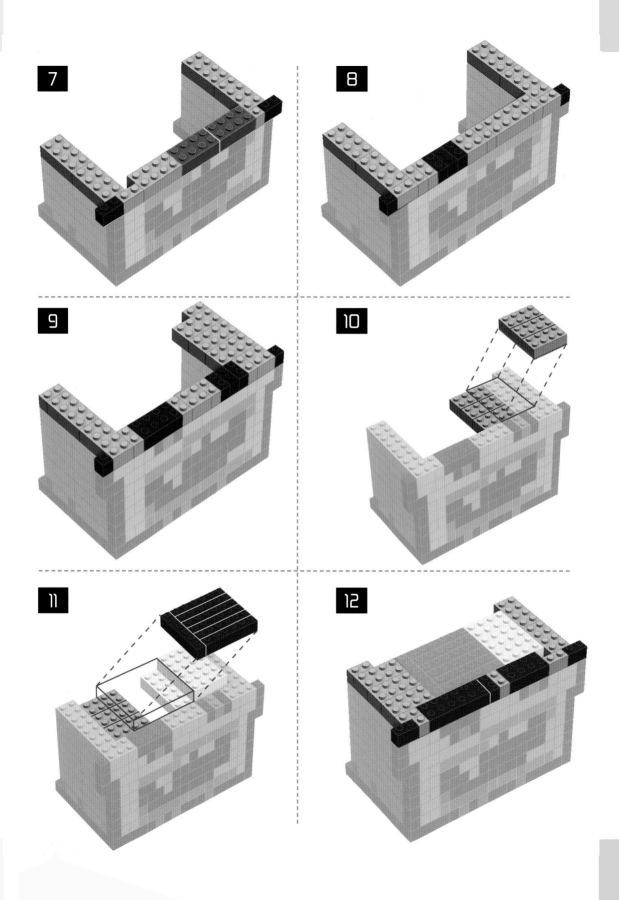

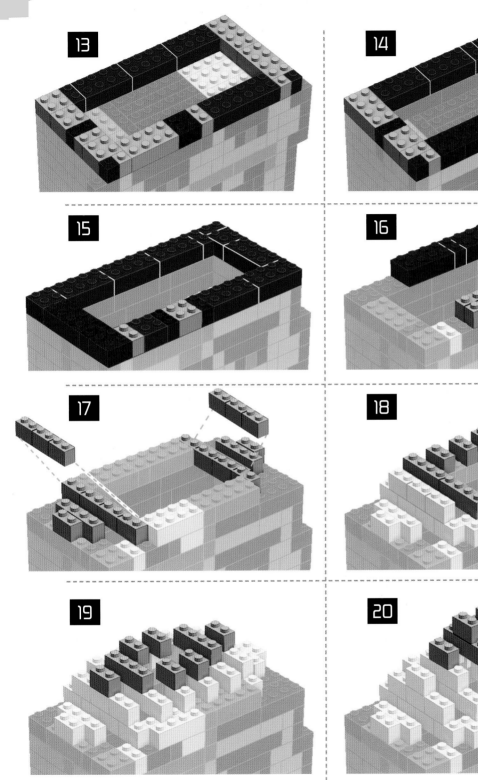

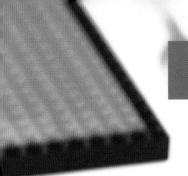

We all have friends whose dinner parties should come with warnings. Why not massively offend them by making a gift of these hazmat mats?

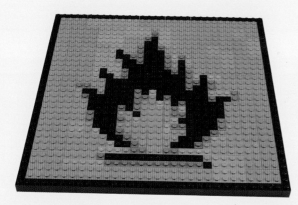

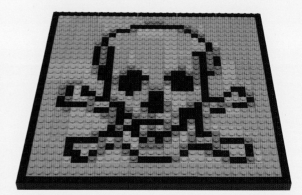

24x
17x
34x
26x
18x
23x
5x
11x
38x

65x
6x
2x

2x

1x   32

32

58x
34x
62x
31x
28x
22x
2x
18x
2x

2x
11x
21x

52x
3x

1x   32

32

FLAMMABLE MAT

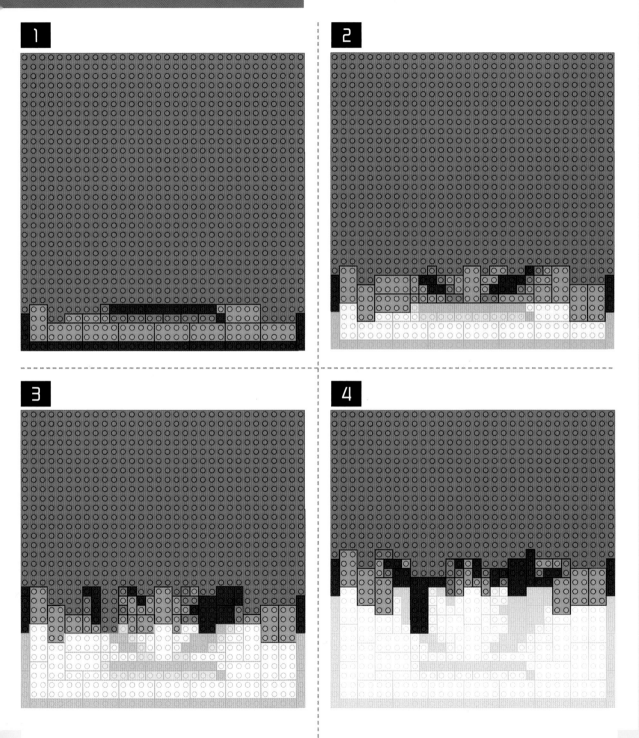

5

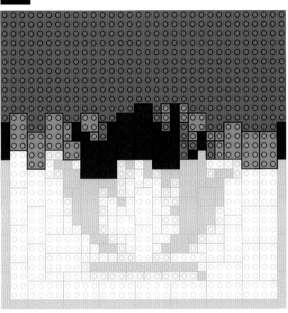

6

7

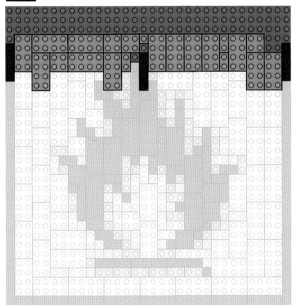

8

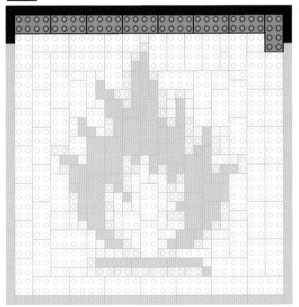

TOXIC MAT

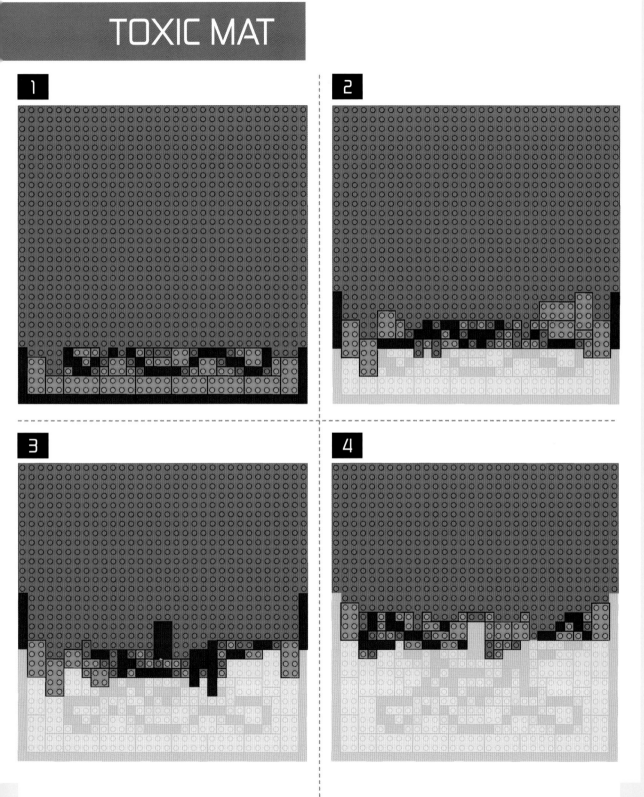

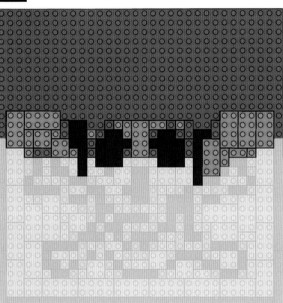

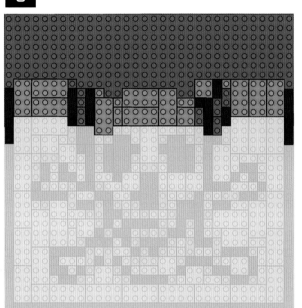

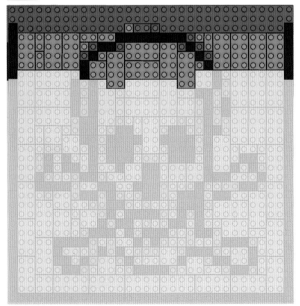

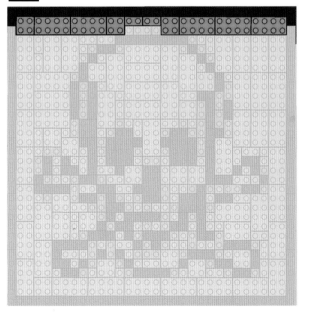

HANGING GHOST

Impress your friends at Halloween with this hanging decoration. More cute than scary, it's the perfect party piece to inject a little humor into the horror.

2x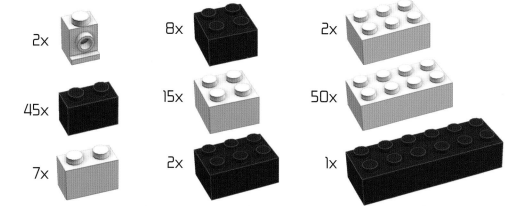

8x

2x

45x

15x

50x

7x

2x

1x

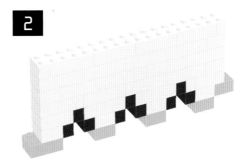

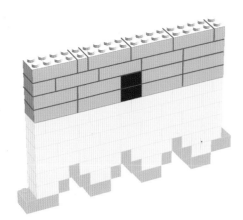

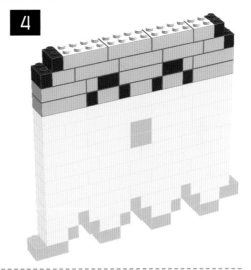

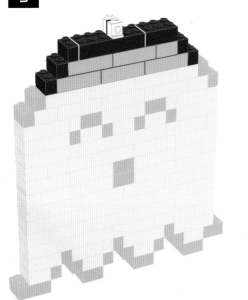

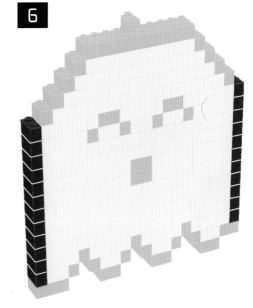

FLOPPY DISK COASTERS

Who says floppy disks are obsolete? Set down your mug and enjoy a byte of lunch with this geeky favorite.

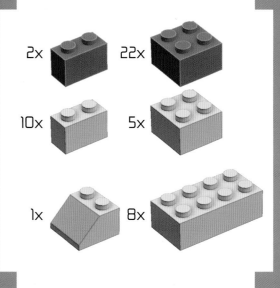

2x
22x
10x
5x
1x
8x

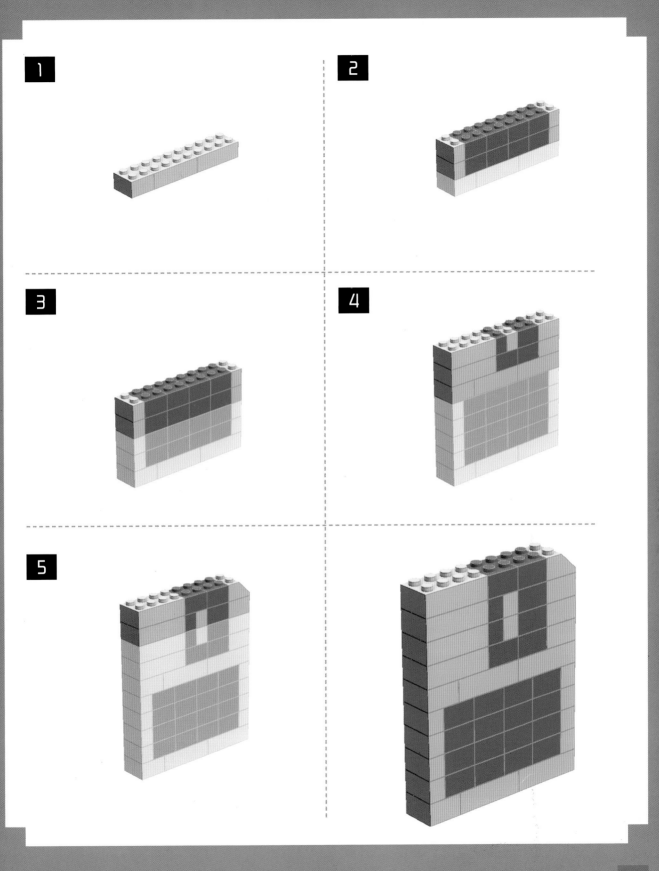

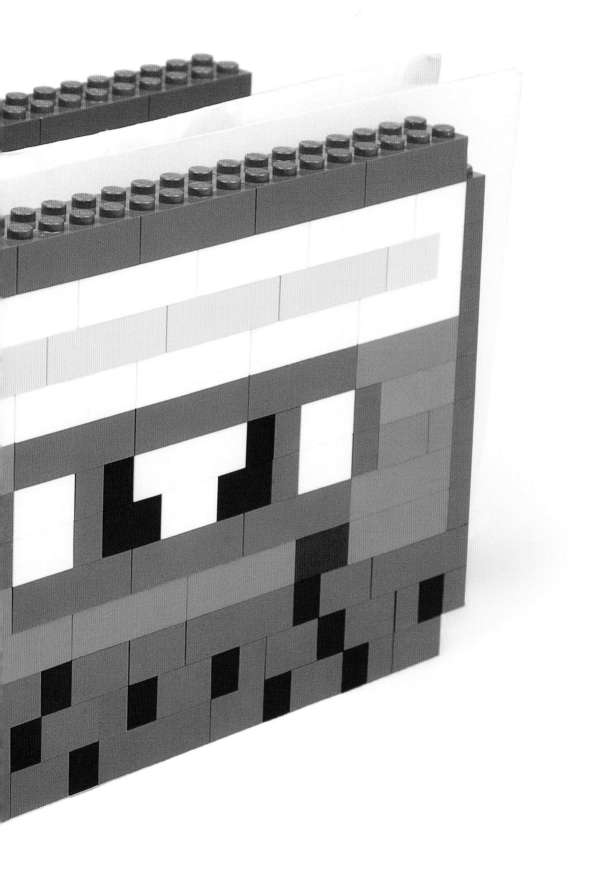

You've heard of a CD rack, but this is oh-so-much better. Why not give your desk space a vintage twist with this audio class?

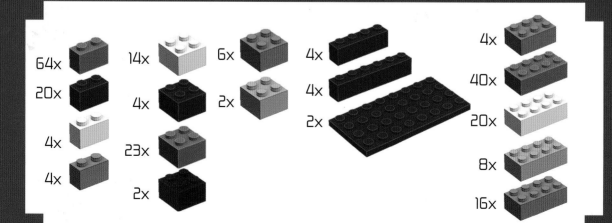

64x
20x
4x
4x

14x
4x
23x
2x

6x
2x

4x
4x
2x

4x
40x
20x
8x
16x

THE BASE

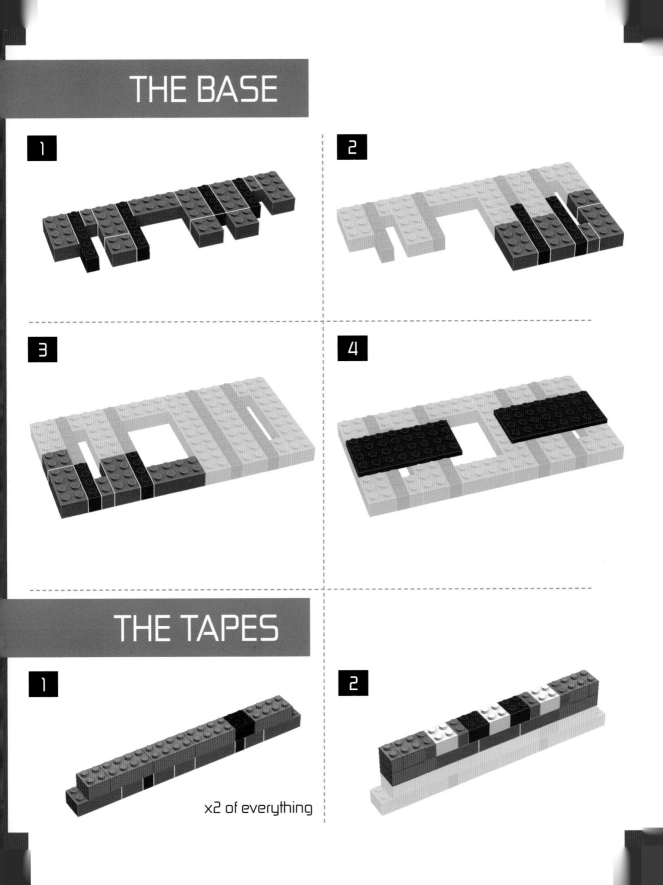

THE TAPES

x2 of everything

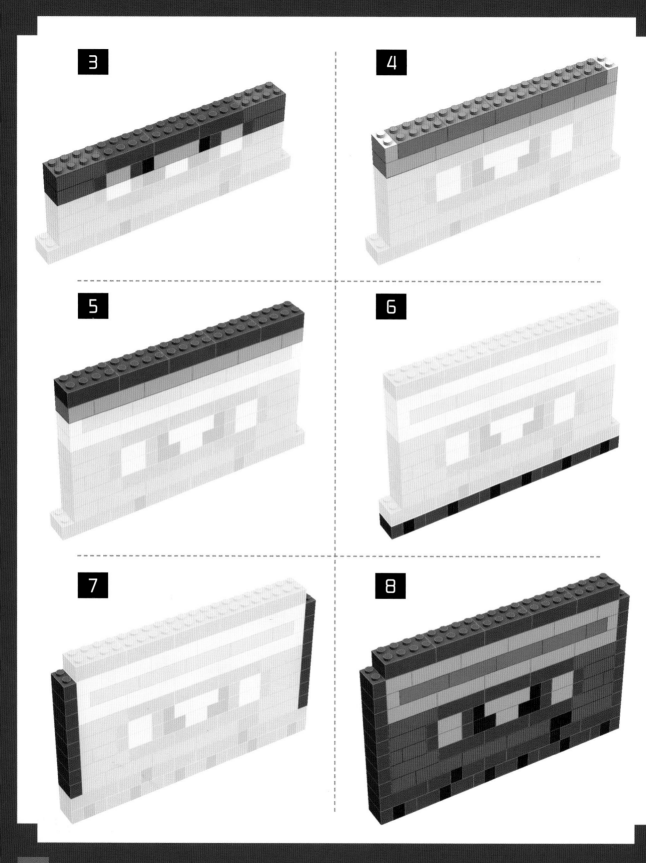

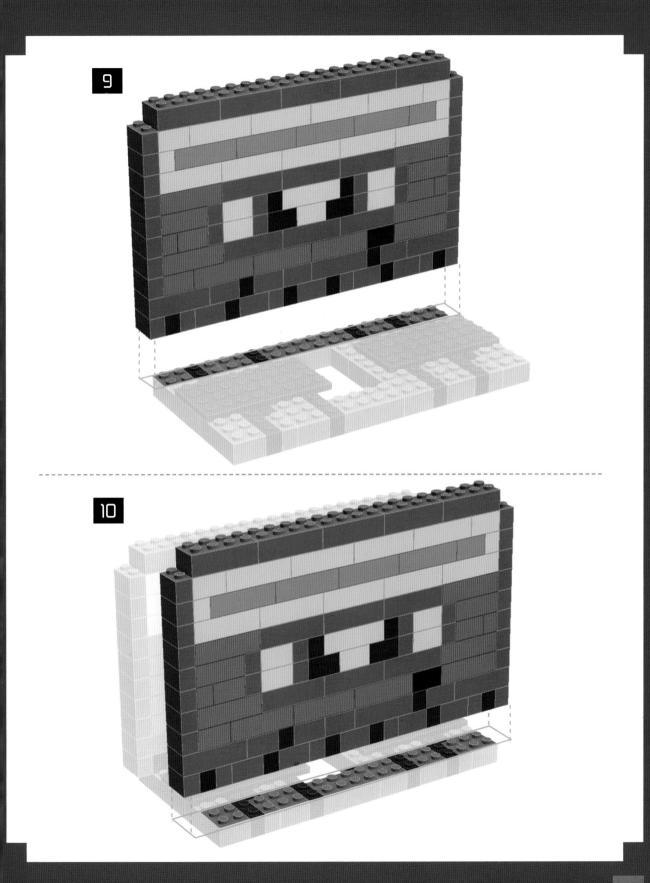

SWORD-IN-THE-STONE PAPERWEIGHT

Prove yourself to be the one true king with this medieval masterpiece, which, when built, will safeguard all your important documents.

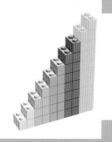

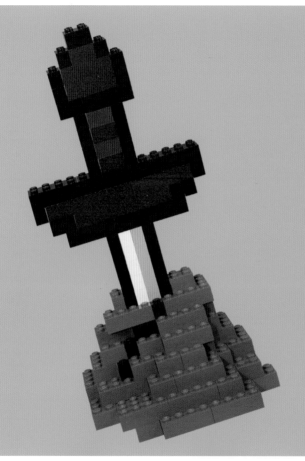

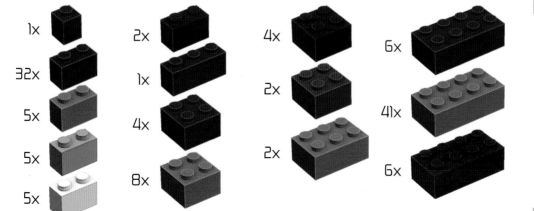

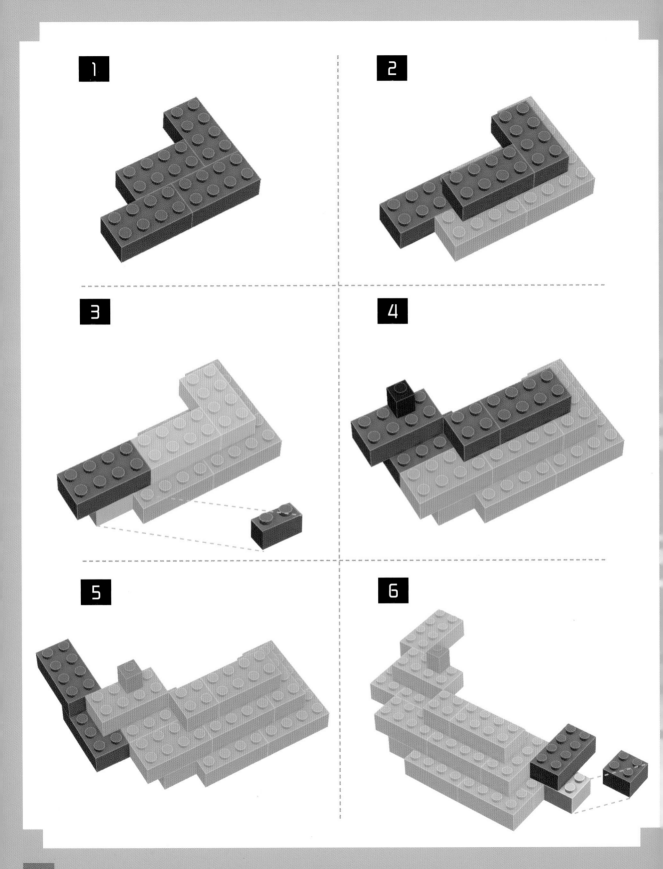

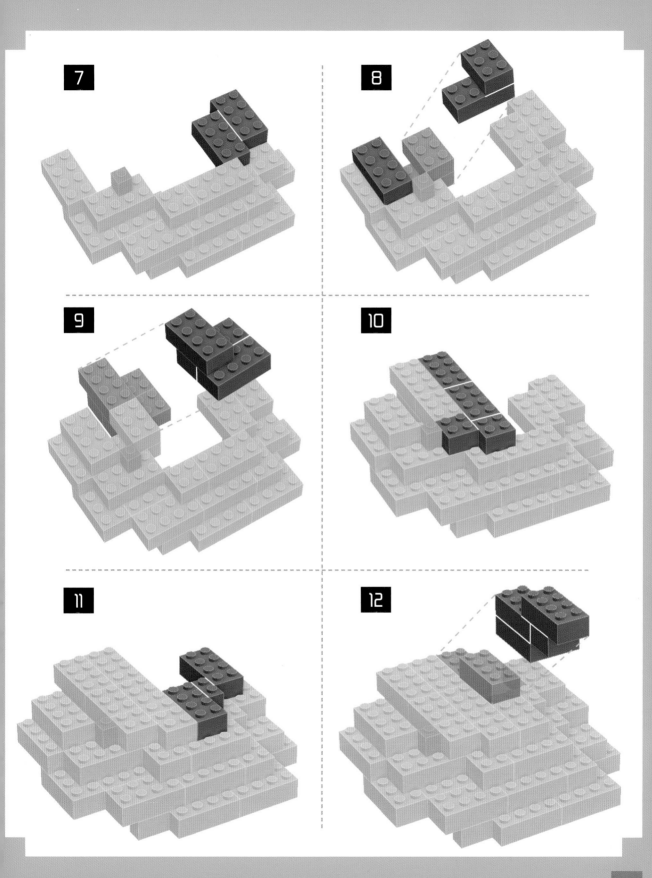

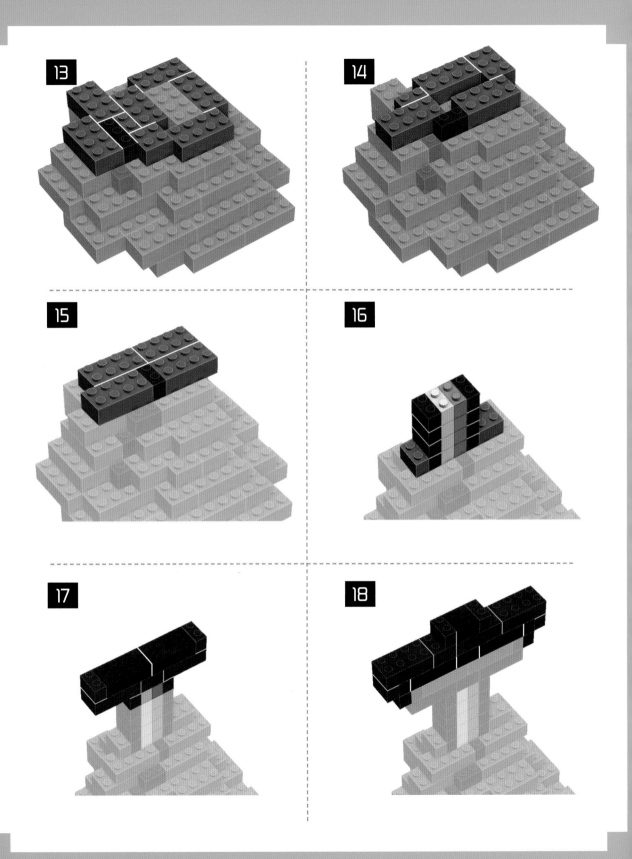

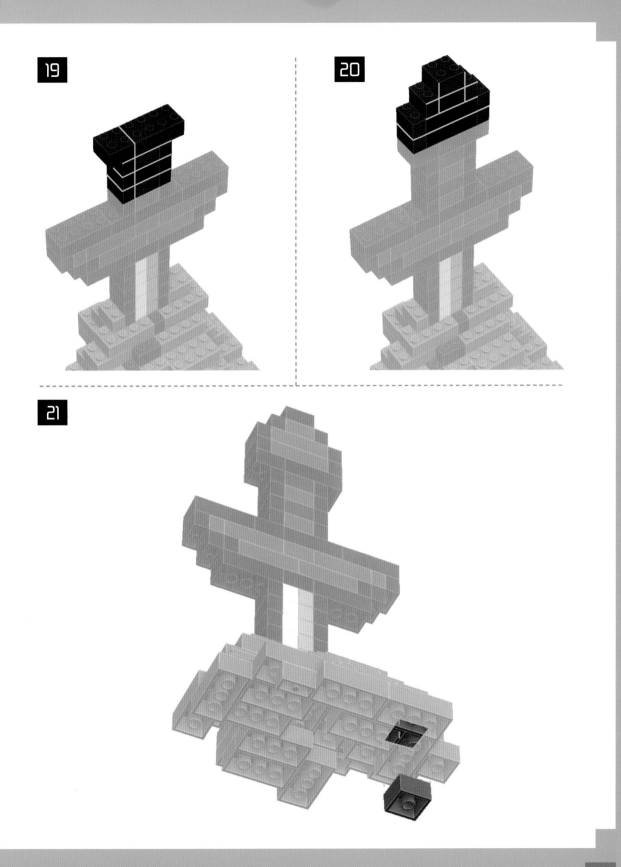

RETRO CONTROLLER PHONE STATION

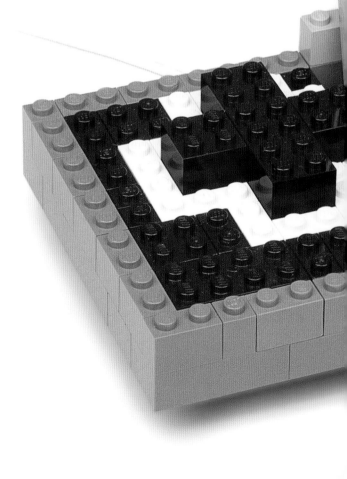

Tap into some nostalgia with this retro controller that doubles as a stand for a charging phone.

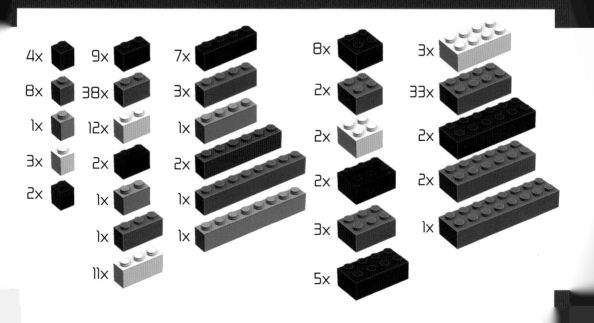

4x
9x
7x
8x
3x

8x
38x
3x
2x
33x

1x
12x
1x
2x
2x

3x
2x
2x
2x
2x

2x
1x
1x
2x
1x

1x
1x
3x

11x
5x

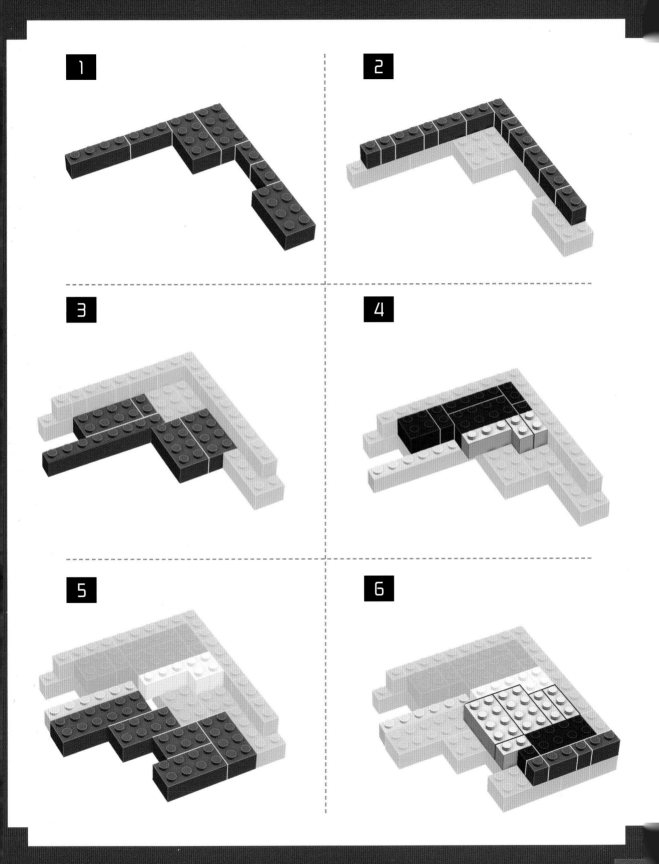

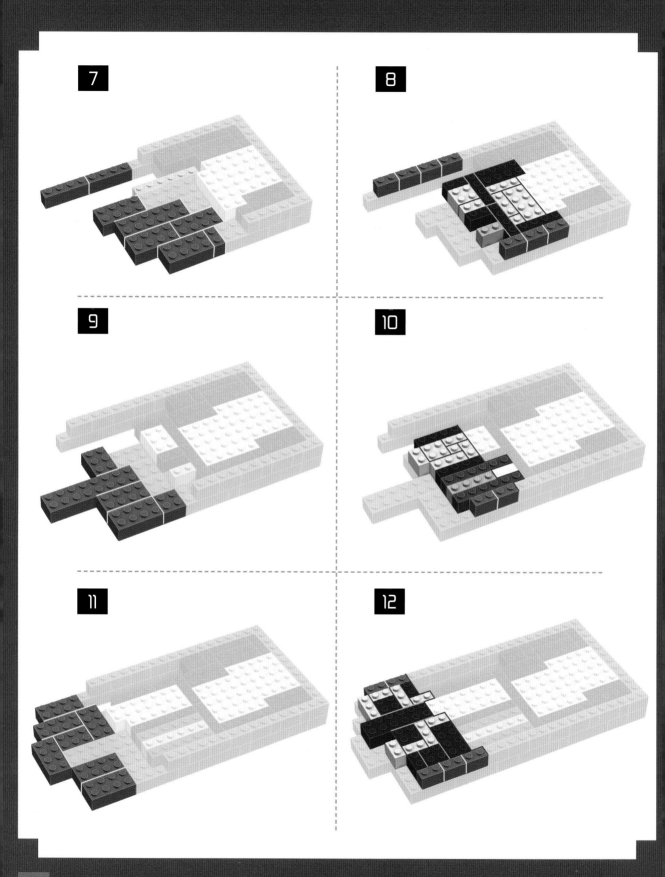

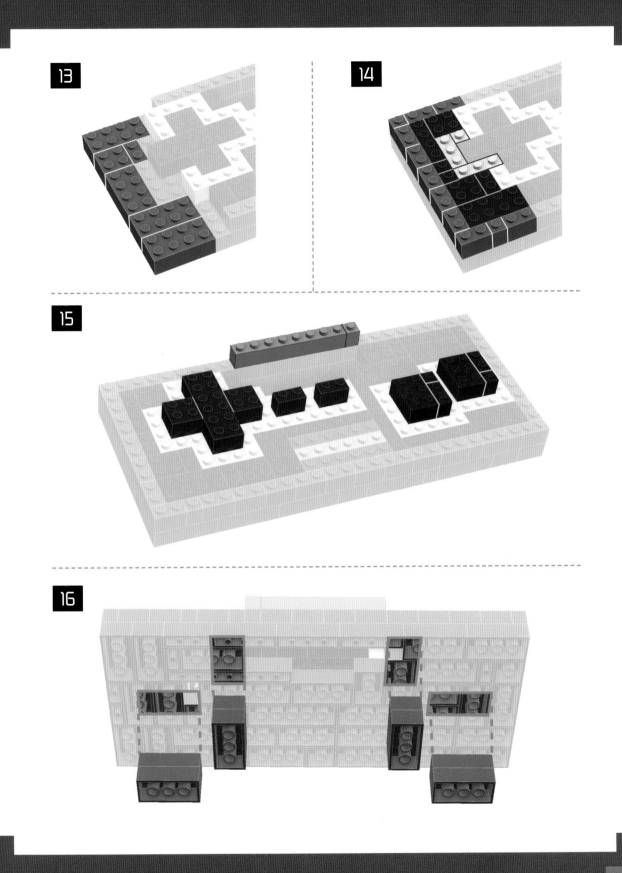

LADY LIBERTY FISH TANK

Get your paws off this icon from the final moments of *Planet of the Apes*. It's just common sense to have a constant reminder of the dangers of our simian brothers.

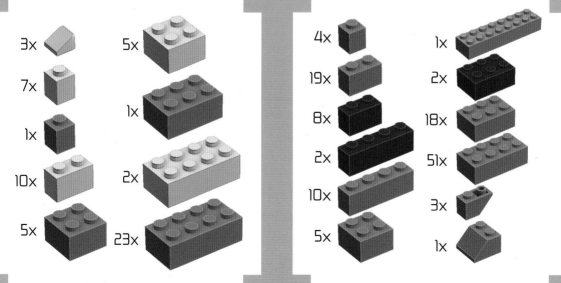

THE HEAD

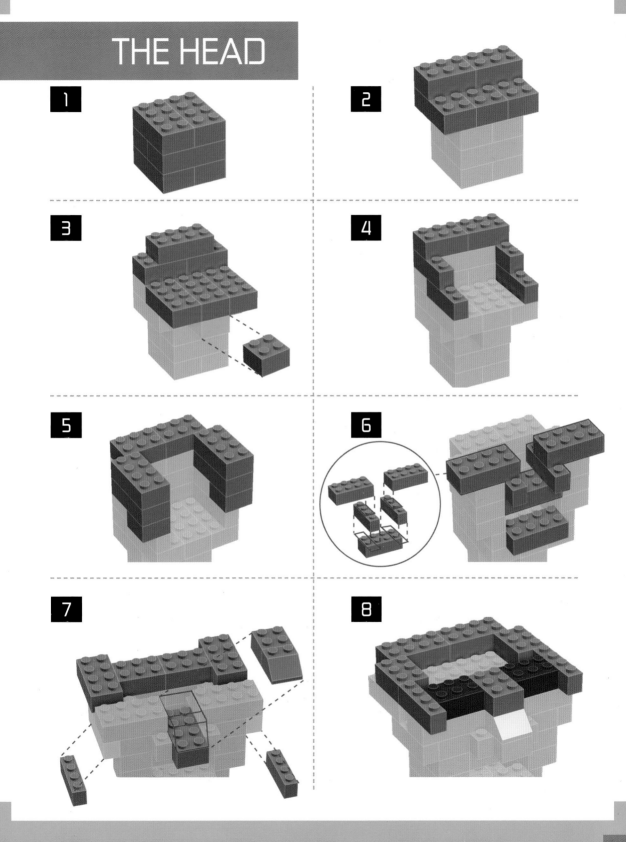

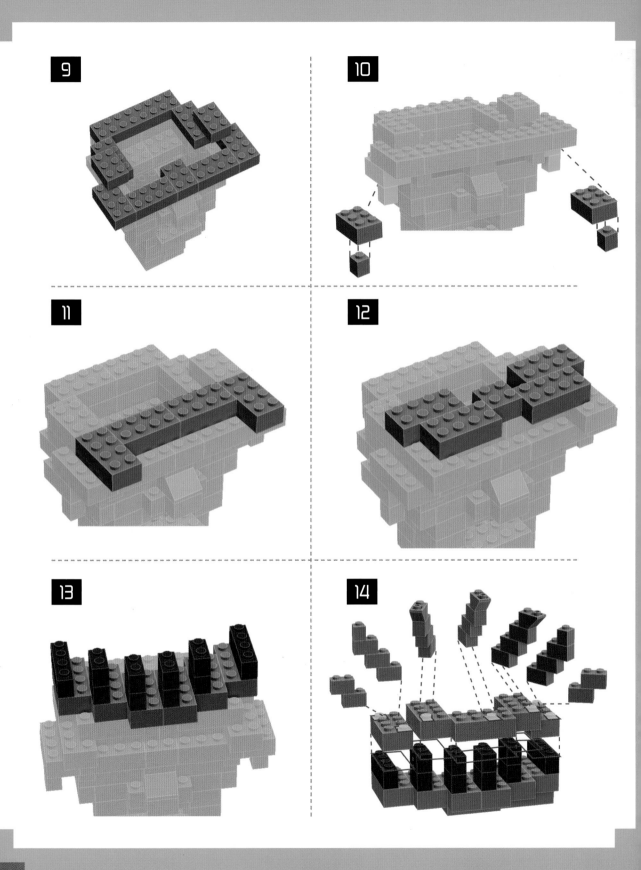

THE TORCH

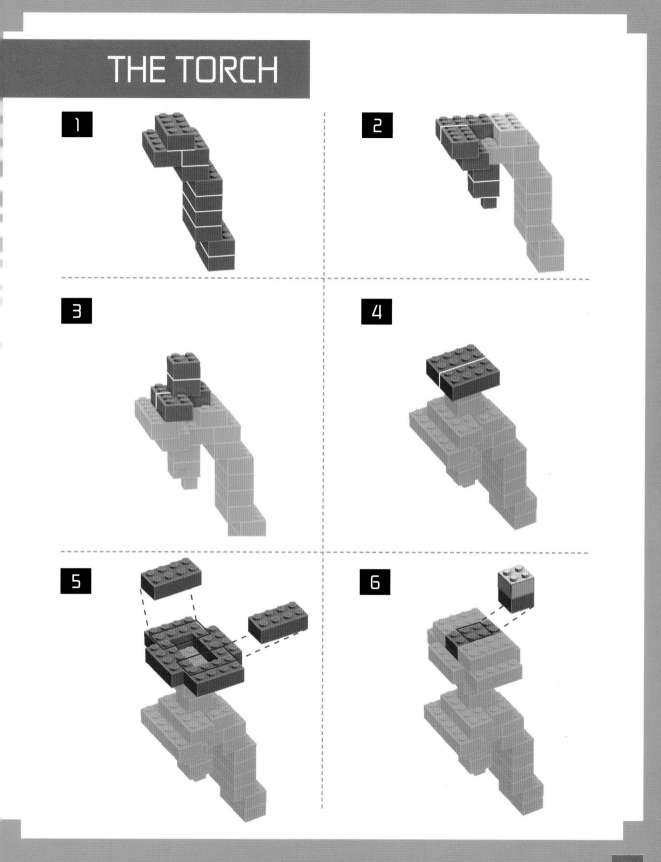

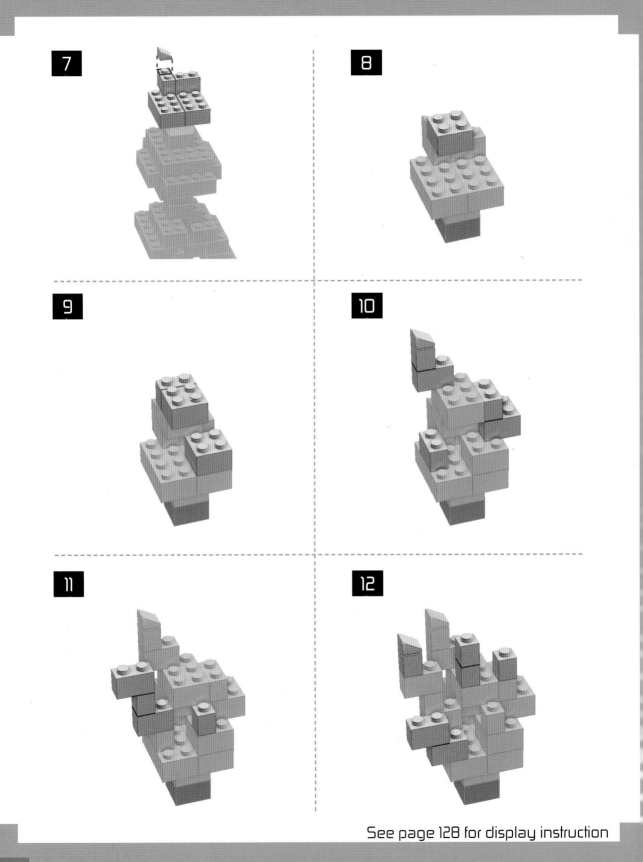

See page 128 for display instruction

"FUZZY" DICE

An update to the 1950s classic, hang these in your car and be the envy of everyone else on the road. That's just how you roll . . .

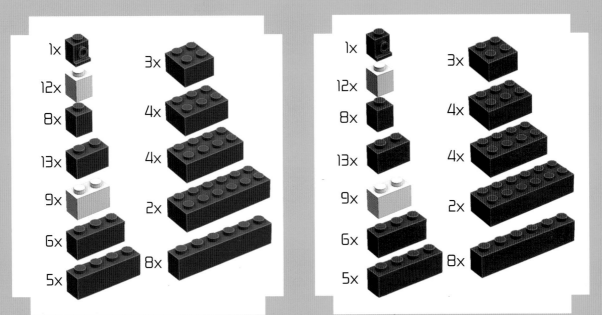

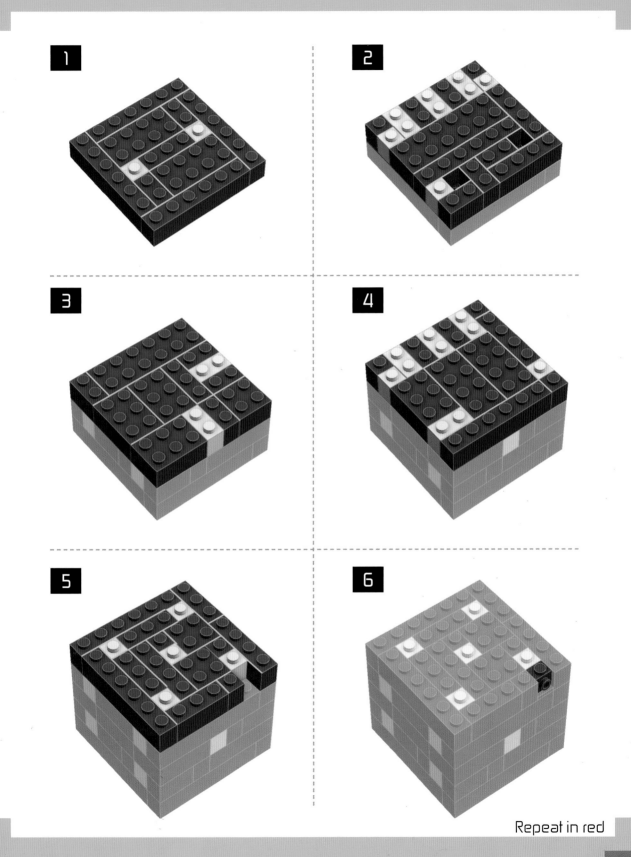

Repeat in red

If you're sick of losing things, then this could be the key to your problems. Use the hooks, or put a Technic brick on your keychain and snap it on!

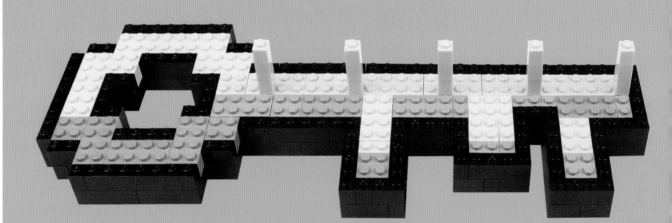

15x
2x
15x
20x
4x
3x

5x
16x
9x
1x
9x

5x
4x
2x
1x

27x
7x
12x
1x

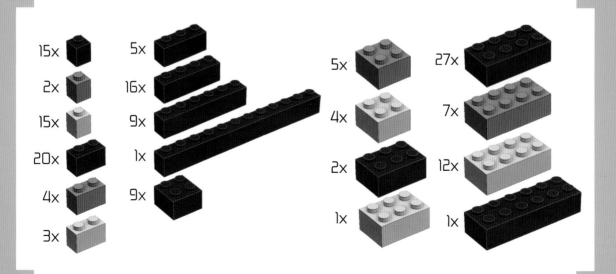

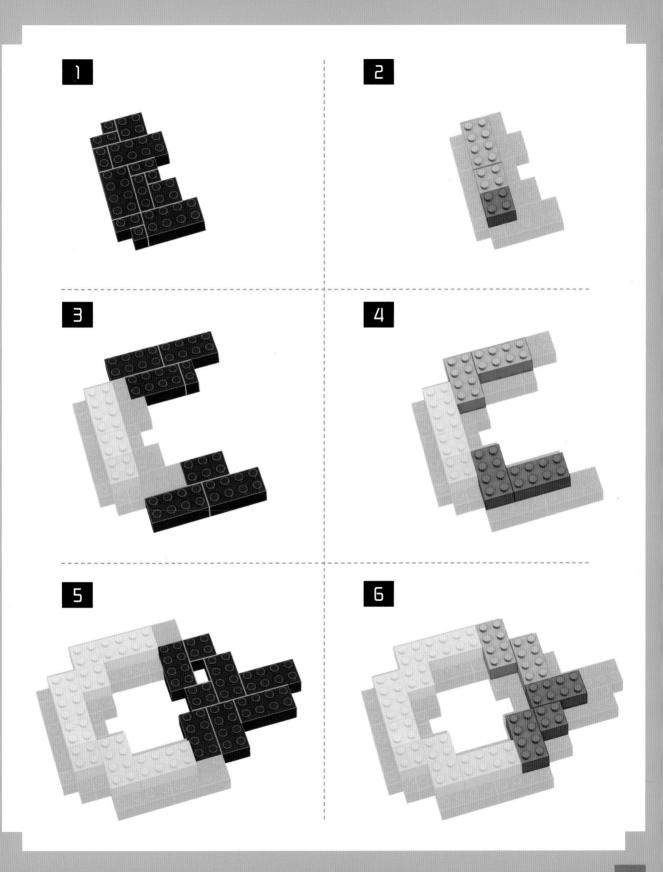

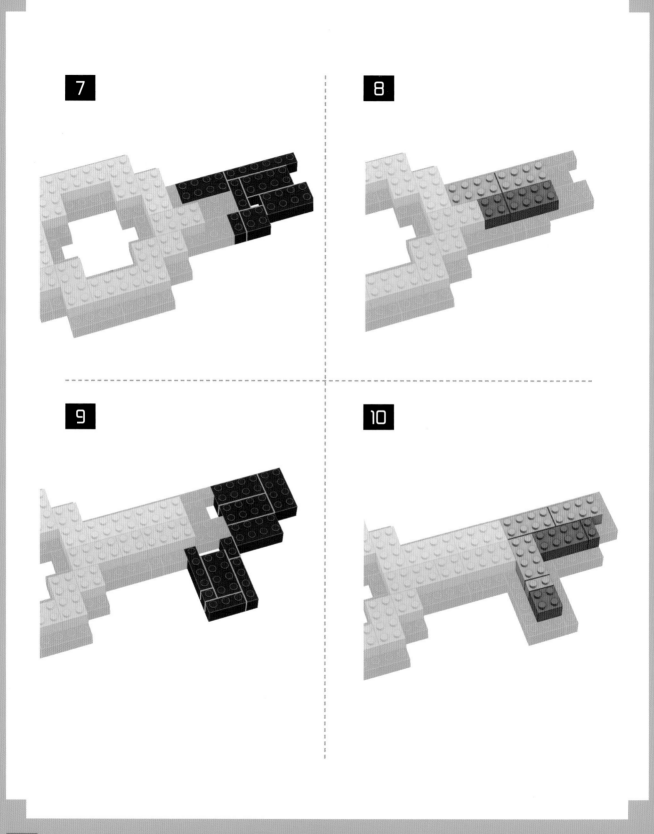

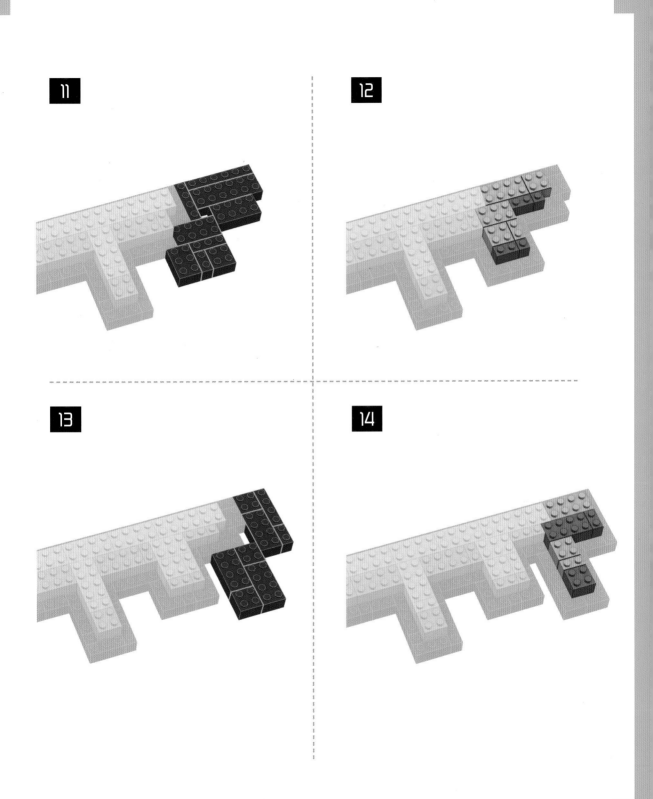

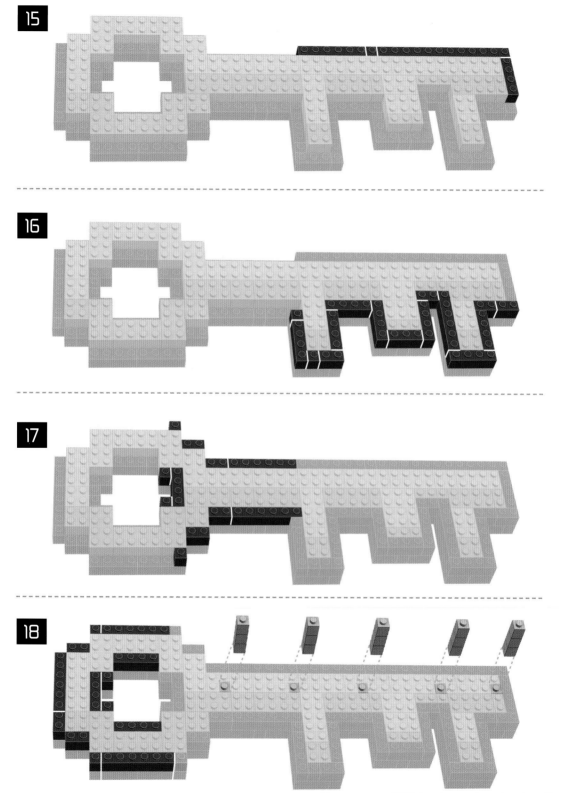

15

16

17

18

See page 128 for hanging instruction

All the thrill of the hunt without any of the blood. Give your home that mountain cabin feel with this bricky trophy. Tricky to construct, but once built, it can hang on your wall and proudly display your status as a LEGO master.

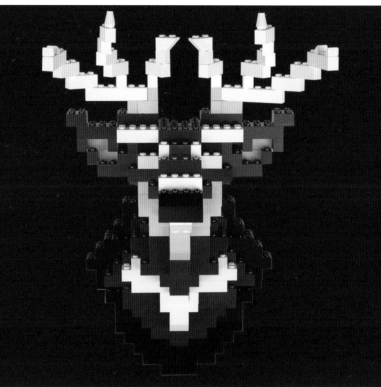

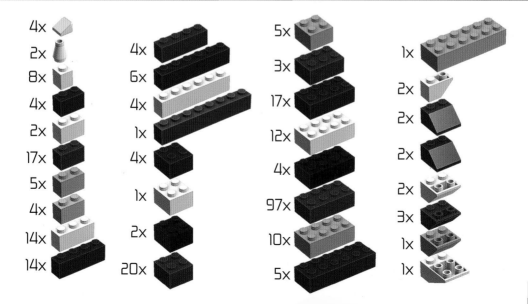

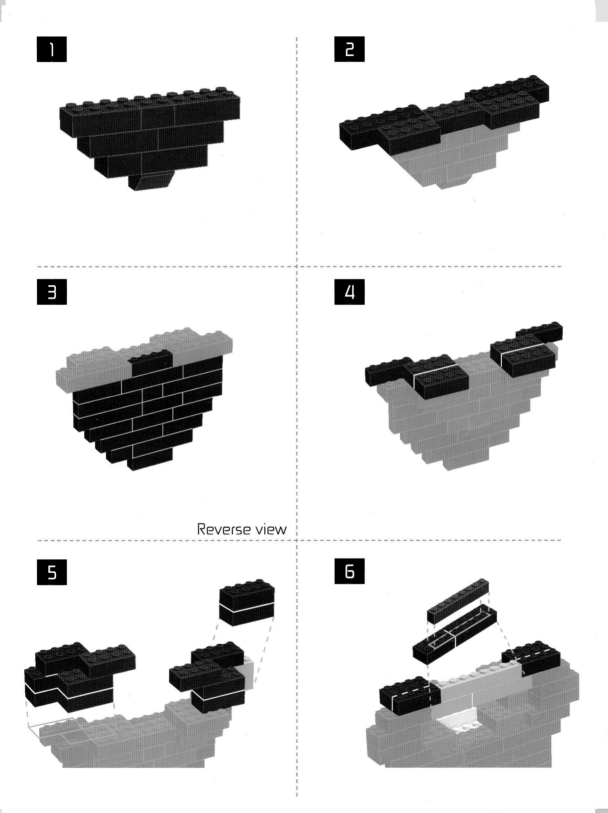

Reverse view

Reverse view

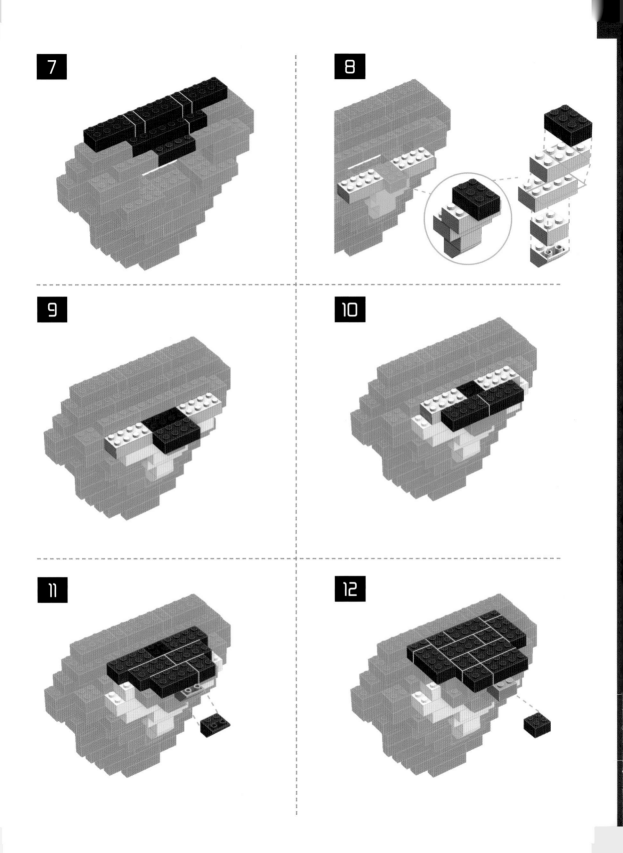

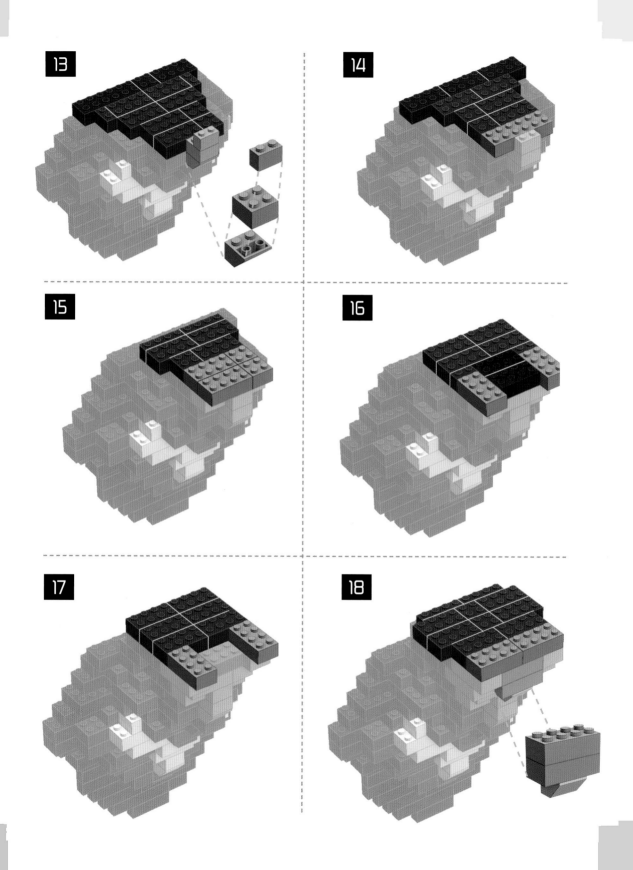

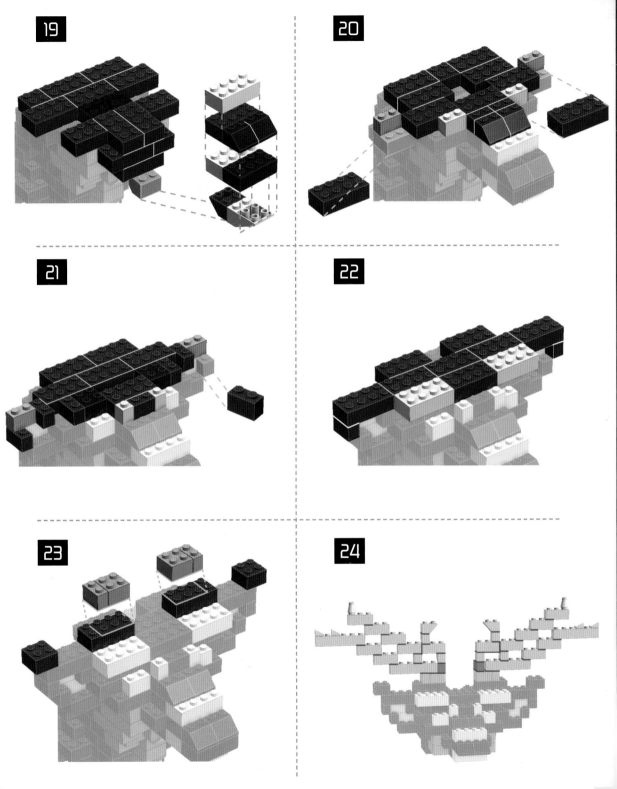

See page 128 for hanging instruction

FRIDGE MAGNETS

Missing the best game of all time? Then bring back memories of this vintage classic. Your fridge has never looked so good.

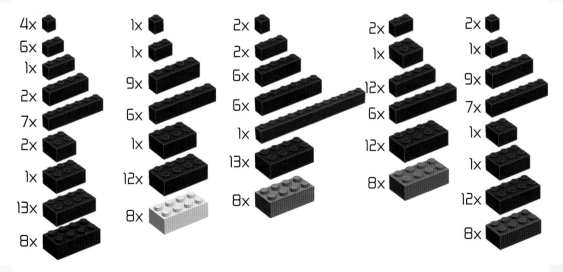

RED BRICKS

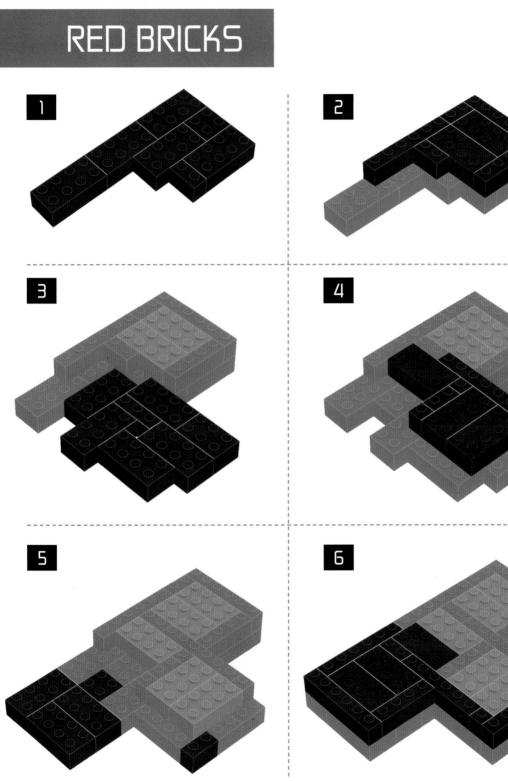

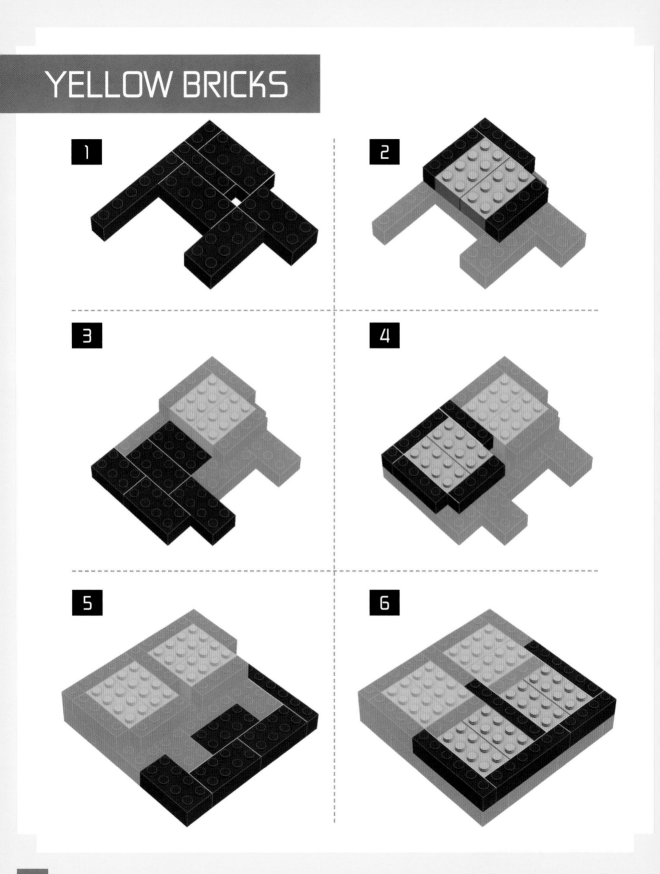

ORANGE BRICKS

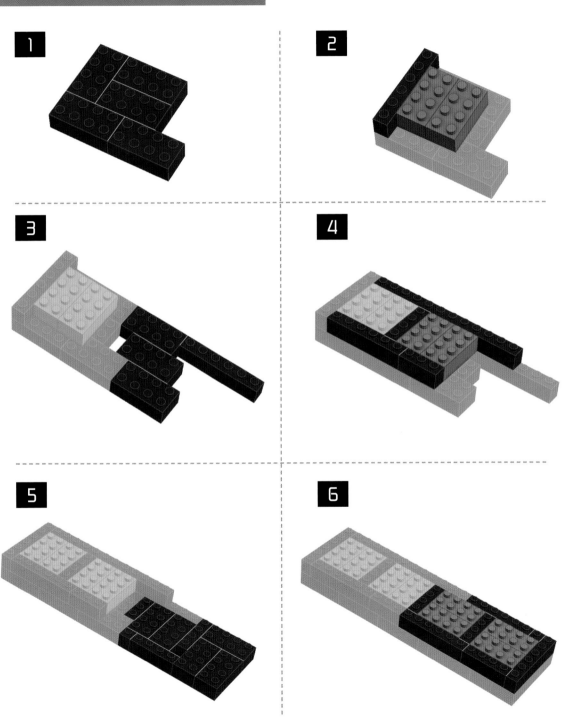

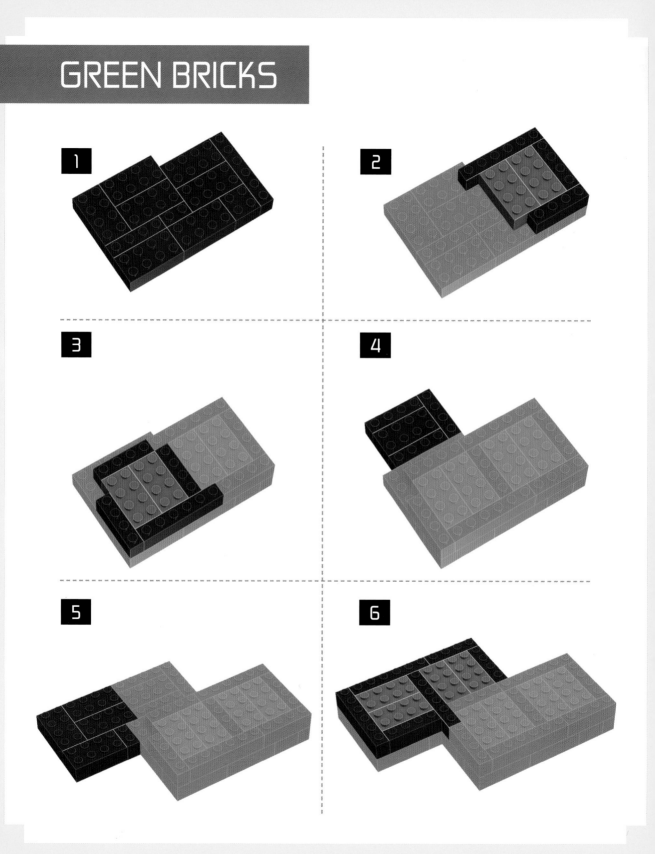

BLUE BRICKS

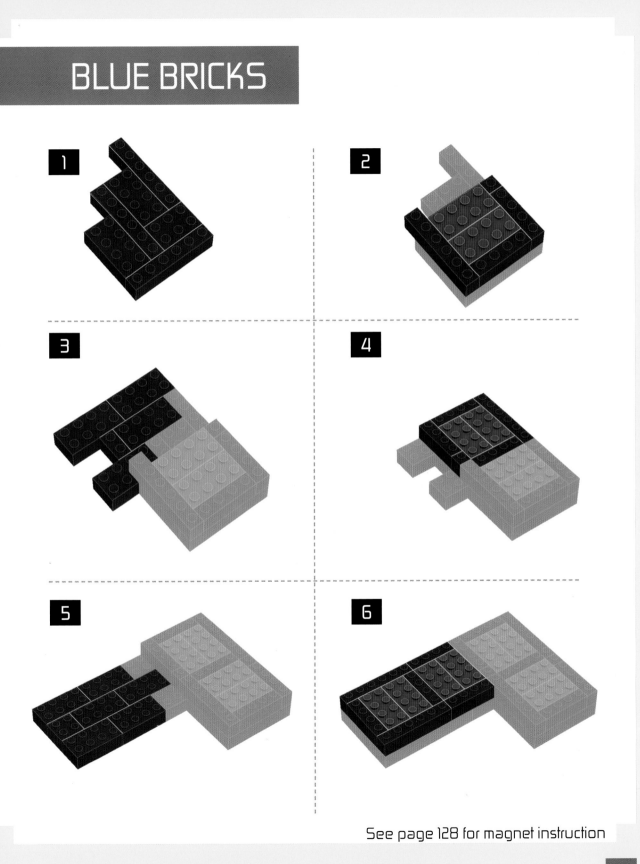

See page 128 for magnet instruction

BEARSKIN RUG

Impress your friends with your very own furry friend. Part trophy, part tray, why not bring a little grizzly to the table?

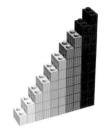

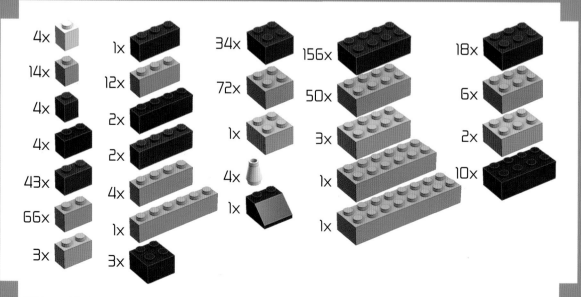

4x
14x
4x
4x
43x
66x
3x

1x
12x
2x
2x
4x
1x
3x

34x
72x
1x
4x
1x

156x
50x
3x
1x
1x

18x
6x
2x
10x

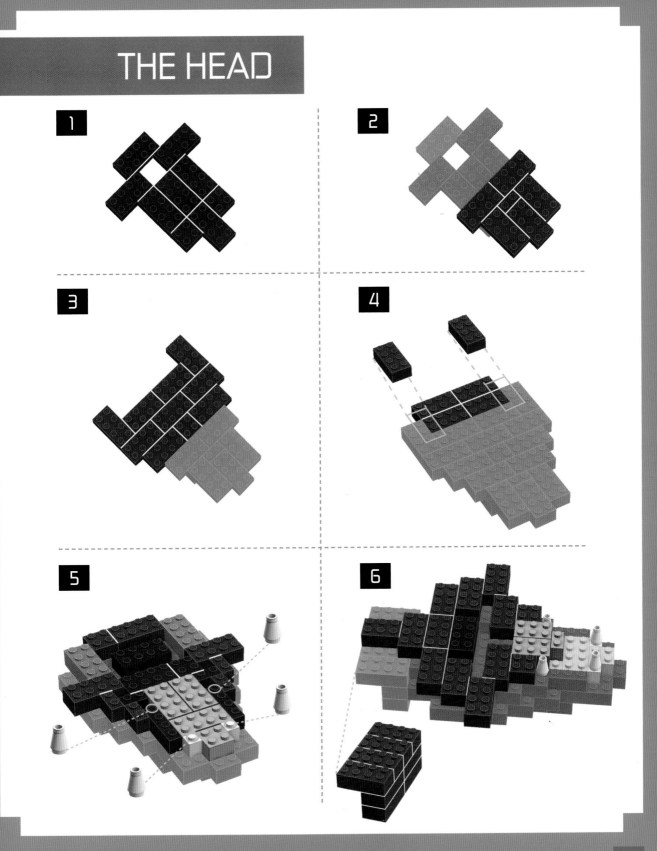

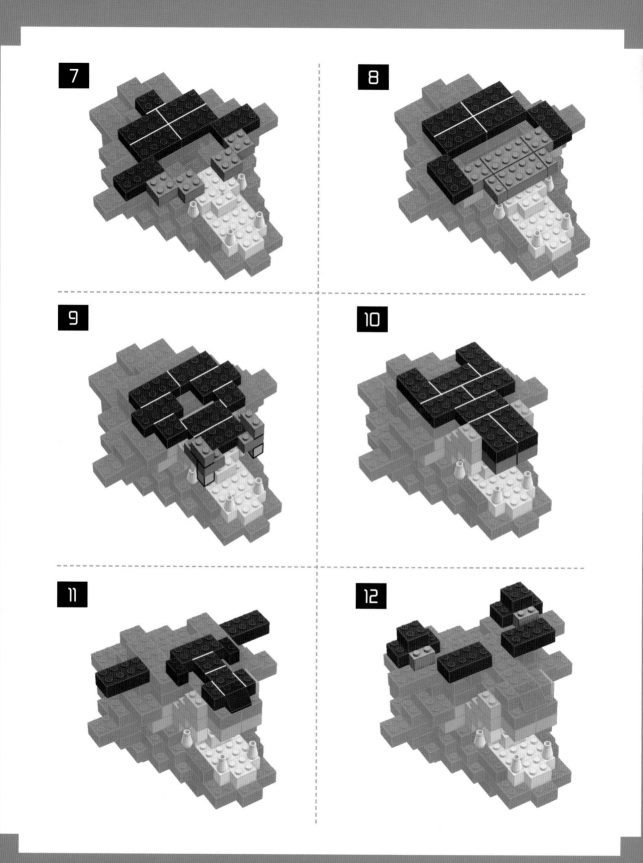

THE BODY

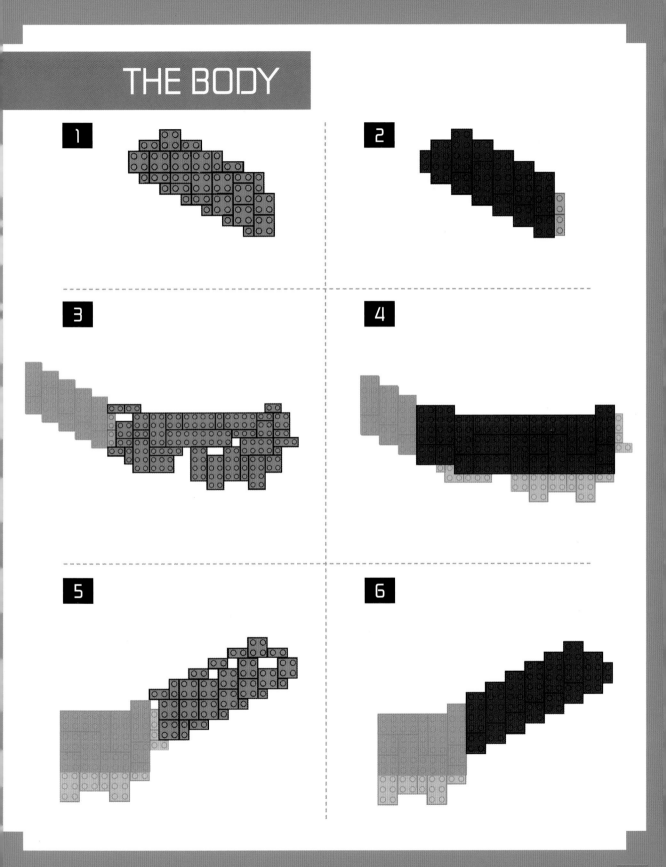

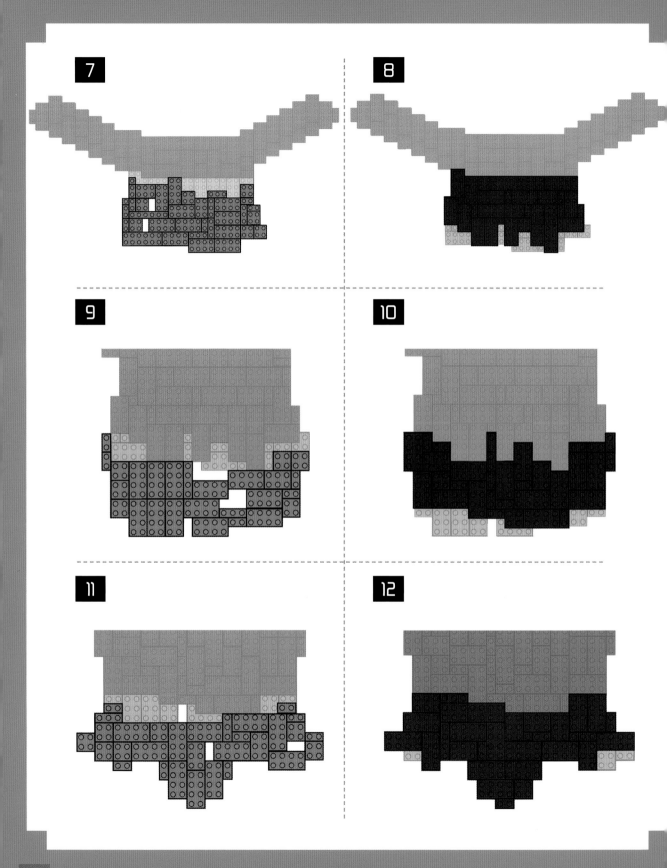

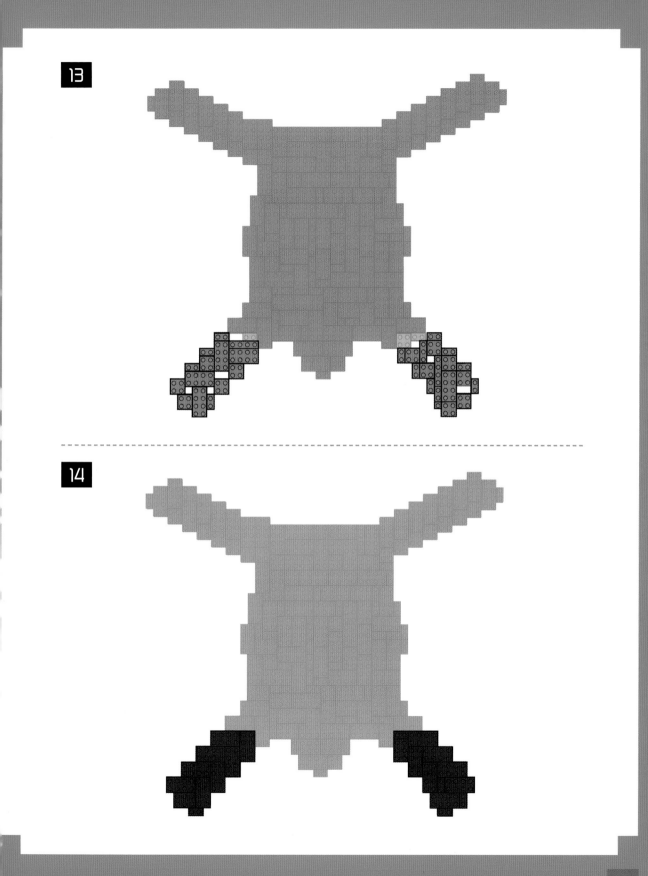

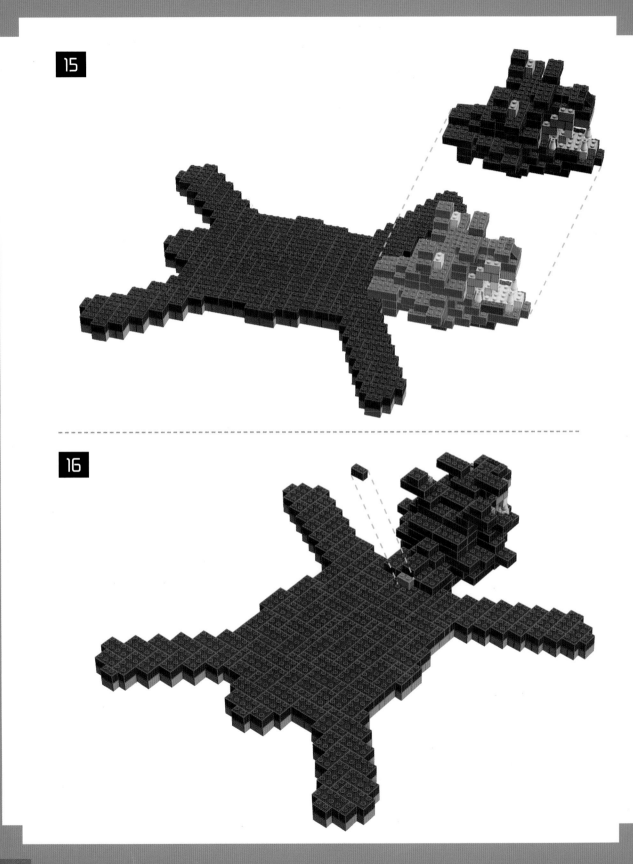

Stand back, she's gonna blow! A little tricky to construct, but well worth it when you have, this volatile vessel is sure to bring some bang to your flower display.

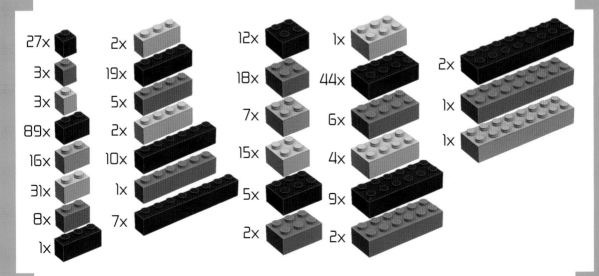

27x
3x
3x
89x
16x
31x
8x
1x

2x
19x
5x
2x
10x
1x
7x

12x
18x
7x
15x
5x
2x

1x
44x
6x
4x
9x
2x

2x
1x
1x

THE BODY

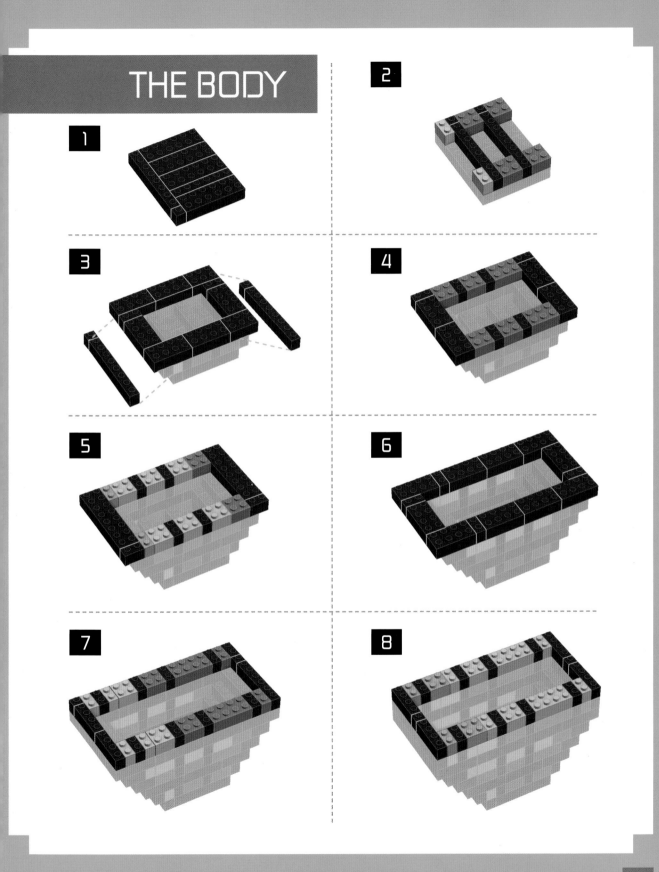

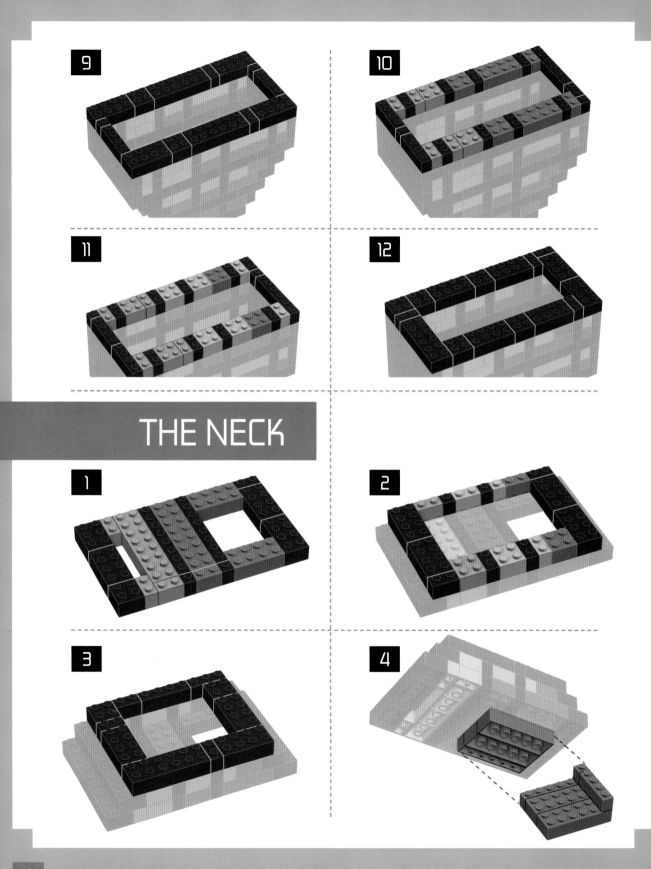

THE NECK

THE POT

1

2

3

THE PIN

1

THE LEVER

1

2

2

3

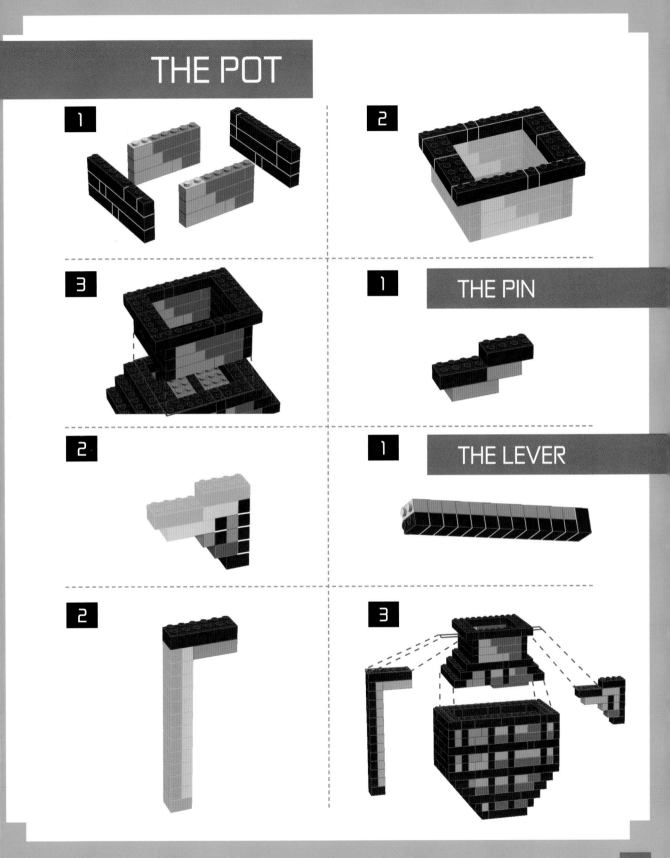

ROBOT WINE BOTTLE HOLDER

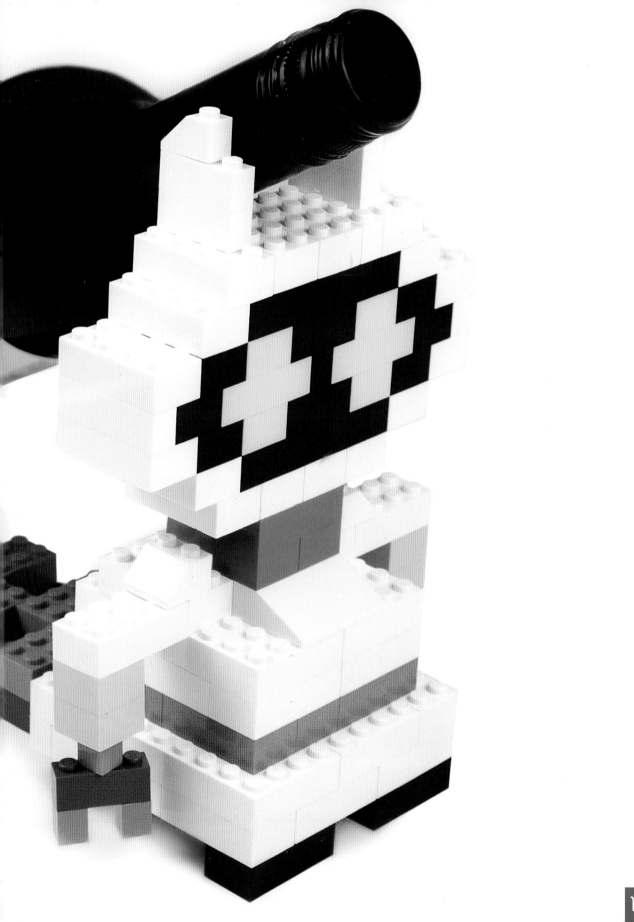

These two 1980s androids are the perfect servants to hold your wine bottle. Fiercely loyal, the boozy bots don't move unless commanded to do so.

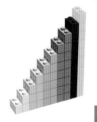

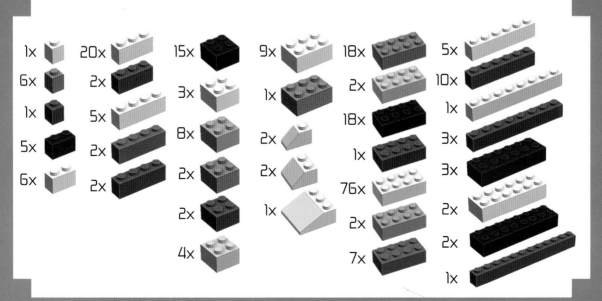

1x   20x   15x   9x   18x   5x

6x   2x   2x   10x

1x   5x   3x   1x   18x   1x

5x   2x   8x   2x   1x   3x

6x   2x   2x   2x   76x   3x

       2x   1x   2x   2x

       4x   7x   2x

                                  1x

SMALL ROBOT

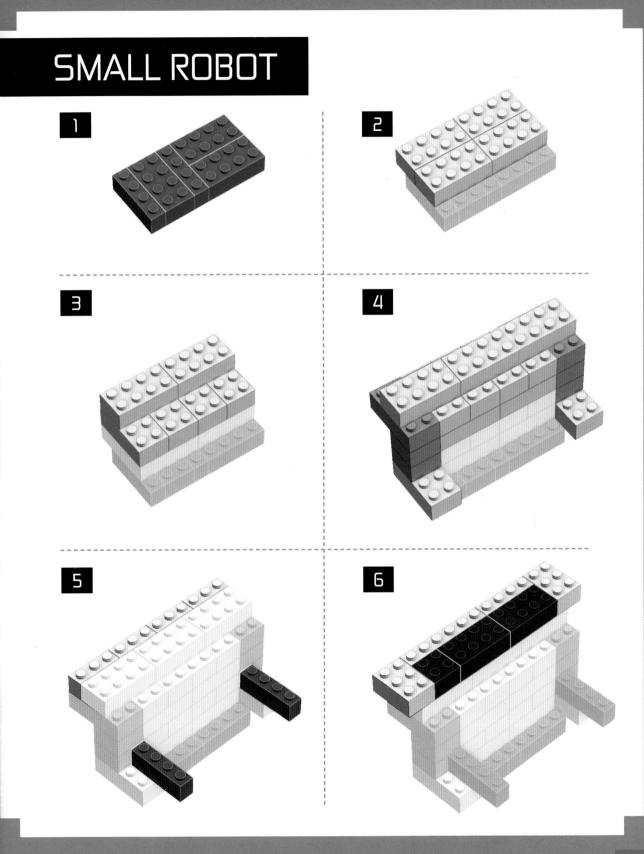

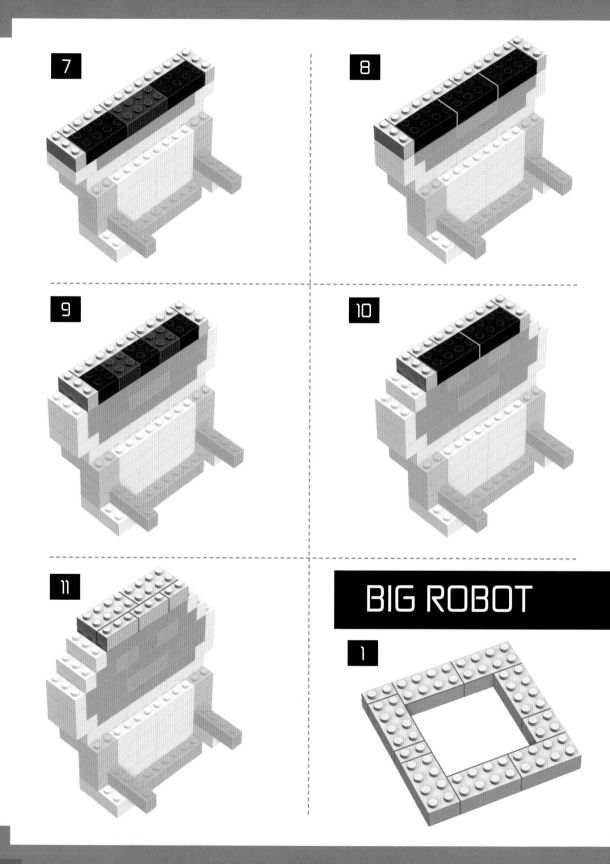

BIG ROBOT

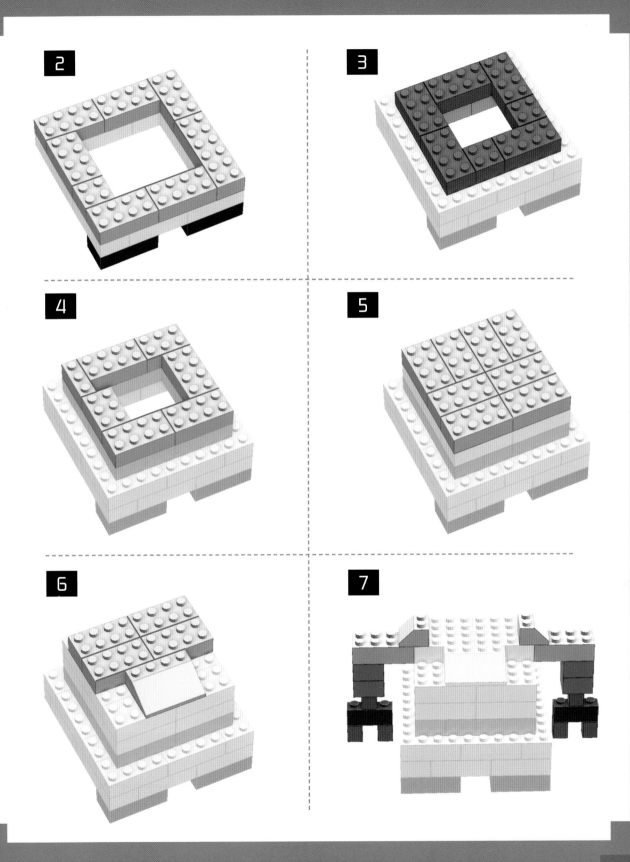

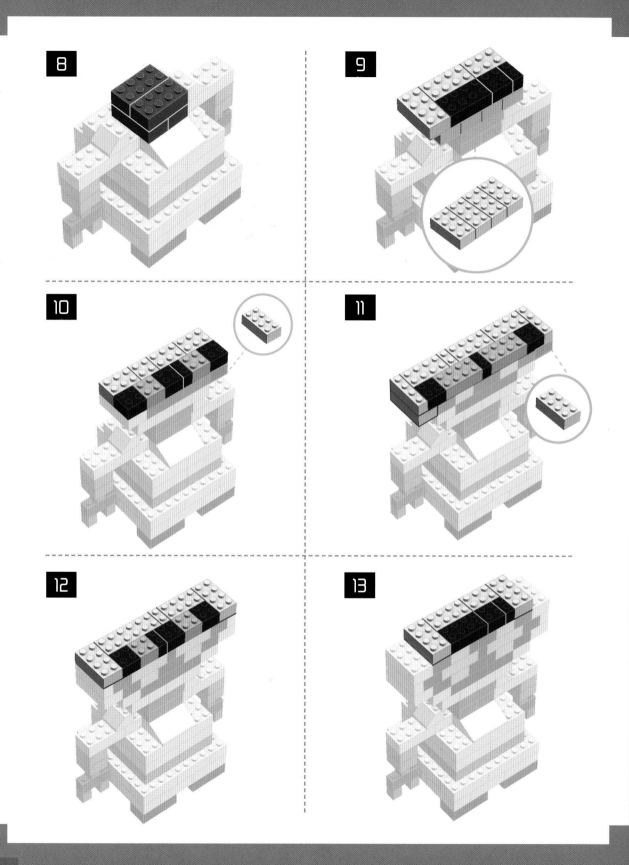

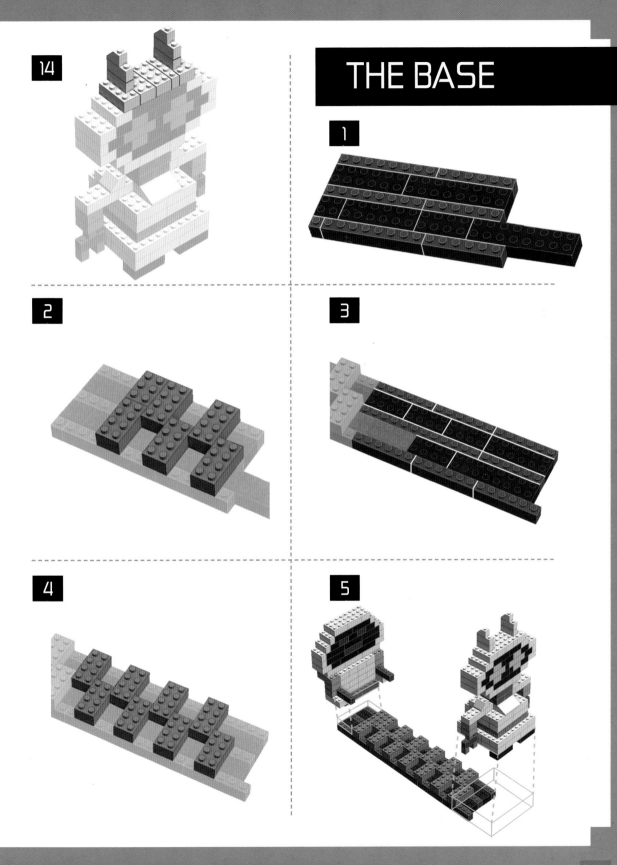

FURTHER INSTRUCTIONS

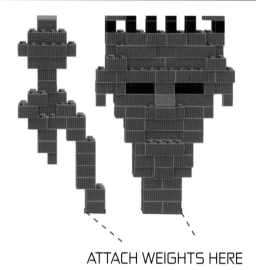

ATTACH WEIGHTS HERE

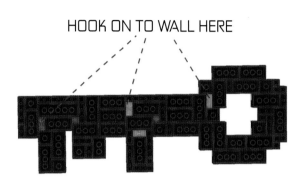

HOOK ON TO WALL HERE

HOOK ON TO WALL HERE

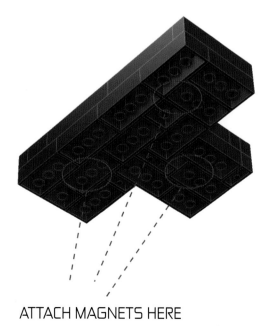

ATTACH MAGNETS HERE